PLOT GARDENING

WRITE FASTER, WRITE SMARTER

CHRIS FOX

CHRIS FOX WRITES, LLC

WRITE FASTER, WRITE SMARTER SERIES

INTRODUCTION

It's been almost a year since I've published a book for writers. For a guy whose claim to fame is writing fast, that might seem odd. I mean, I talk about publishing a book a month. So where are the books, Chris?

In 2017 I made a conscious decision to really double down on craft. I wanted to master story and to really understand what made it work, why some of my novels blew up, and why others had mediocre sales. Some would argue that marketing was the key, and don't get me wrong, that's part of it. That's why the last four books in the series all touch on marketing.

But at its heart, what really sells our book is the content. **It's the story.** It is infinitely easier to sell a great story than it is a mediocre one. So, it's time this series added some craft, and taught the hard-won lessons I've teased out of the publishing world over the last few years.

I'm entirely too proud to say that over 250,000 people have paid for one of my books in some form, across fifteen novels and the previous six books in this series. The vast majority of those sales come from novels, with *Destroyer* and *Tech Mage* holding the top spots.

Both novels were Plot Gardened, though if you'd asked me at the time I wouldn't have been able to tell you that's what I was doing. I'll explain exactly what that term means in the next chapter, but the short version is that Plot Gardening is a bridge between 'by the seat of your pants' writing and meticulous plotting. Both have their place, as you'll see in the pages that follow.

I know many people reading are like me when reading a book like this, and simply don't care about the author. If that's you, have a high five as you skip right on to Chapter 1, where the real learning starts.

… For those curious, though, here's a bit about me.

When I started this series with *5,000 Words Per Hour* back in June of 2015, I was still a software engineer working in San Francisco. Every morning I'd hop on the #54 bus from Novato, and spend the next hour to hour and a half writing as we bounced our way toward the financial district.

I published five books during 2015, but by February of 2016 I realized it was too much to sustain alongside a full-time job. I had a difficult decision. Either I needed to scale back publishing, or I needed to give up the day job.

So I quit the day job.

I didn't do it willy-nilly. I saved up a year's worth of income, and I paid off all my debt. I also made damned sure my books were selling before I pulled the plug. It was one of the scariest decisions I've ever made.

When the dust settled at the end of 2016 I could truly claim to be a six-figure author, and had that honor again at the end of 2017. This writer thing is brutally hard, but wow can it be rewarding. I've spoken in Florida, Vegas, and will be in Chicago and Seattle to speak this year. Next year I'll be speaking in Bali at the 20Books conference.

This strange journey is leading me all over the world, and introducing me to some amazing authors. I've watched many of those authors use my *Write to Market* methodology to blow away my income. I've studied their success, and looked at my own.

My conclusion? There's going to be an explosion of content in the next decade. More and more people are realizing that self-publishing is profitable, and they want their piece of the pie. I saw the same thing happen in the app world.

If we want to survive, we do that by being the best authors in our genre. We win loyal readers, and that battle is fought with story. It's entirely dependent on our craft, and that's why I wrote this book. It's the culmination of my quest to master story, because I understand it's vital to my career as an author.

To that end, I read every book available on plotting, outlining, or storytelling. I re-watched all of Campbell's and Sanderson's videos, and videos of random YouTube personalities. I binged everyone from John Truby to K.M. Weiland to John McKee.

More importantly, I experimented. I've got fifteen novels in print, and each one benefited from the previous book. Each time I tried something new, and learned a little more. Now I finally feel ready to share what I've learned.

It's my hope that this book helps you take your craft to the next level, and that you write the next great novel that delights me the same way other greats have. Either way, it's a privilege to share this journey with you.

Chris Fox
February, 2018

PART I

FOUNDATION

PLOT GARDENING

Have you ever given up sleep to finish a book? Or been walking through Walmart and found yourself stopping to watch an iconic scene in one of your favorite movies? Great stories pull us in and refuse to let us go. They speak to everything that makes us human. They force us to confront our worst fears, and to consider things from entirely different points of view.

These stories shape us as people, and play a role in who we become and how we live our lives. This book is going to teach you how to tell that kind of story, and we're going to do it without sacrificing your creativity.

Some writers will tell you that you need an outline. Others will argue that they need to be unfettered by such things, and cannot write under that kind of constraint. These two groups have self-divided into plotters and pantsers, so named because the latter write by the seat of their pants.

I've claimed to be both over the course of my career, but it wasn't until a year ago that I *realized* I'm both. I meticulously outline novels, but some of my best characters and best scenes have come from discovery writing, or suddenly veering off outline.

After realizing that, I've finally created a third alternative to either rigid plotting, or total freeform writing.

So what is Plot Gardening?

Writing a novel is a massive undertaking, and one that takes most of us a season or longer to do. The title of this book is a play on the two most common methods, borrowed from a Brandon Sanderson lecture.

He claimed that some writers are architects, and others are gardeners. The architects plot out everything meticulously, and know exactly where their stories are going. The gardeners sprinkle some seeds in their subconscious dirt, and wait for something to sprout.

If you'd have asked me ten years ago, I would have said I was a gardener. If you'd have asked me three years ago, I would have said I was an architect. Today, I'm a plot gardener.

I realized that while Sanderson's architect analogy made sense, it left out an important part of the creative process. It stripped away some of the organic creativity that has resulted in my best work.

At the same time, just sprinkling some seeds in the dirt and waiting usually resulted in me staring at a blank cursor. Total creative freedom led to inaction, and then me turning off the laptop and watching Netflix.

Then it dawned on me. The solution involved both routes. A gardener doesn't sprinkle seeds and then just hope. They plant specific seeds. They use the right kind of soil. And smart gardeners may use pesticide or planter boxes. They know how often and how much water to give their seeds.

If you think of your novel as a garden, then the outline is a guide pole you stick in the dirt to direct the growth of plants. The soil is your world building, and your characters are the seeds. Your outline gives them a direction to grow, but how they grow is often organic, and sometimes entirely unpredictable. I am a die-hard outliner, but outlining doesn't even begin until I've been chewing on a plot for a while.

It's this combination of structure and creativity that has helped me write my best novels, and will continue to help me grow as a writer. Over the next few chapters we'll be creating your planter box and your soil, and adding the first few seeds. Before we do, let's talk more about what I mean by soil.

The Accretion Method

Back in my 9th grade earth science class we learned about accretion. Rivers will gradually deposit sediment along riverbanks, always adding new layers over time. This results in incredibly rich soil, and is part of why Egypt was one of the first powerhouses in the ancient world.

We're going to harness the same process to fertilize our gardens. At the end of this chapter, you'll be creating a sort of virtual planter box to hold your novel. My planter box is a Scrivener document. Yours might be a stack of index cards.

Once you have an idea for your novel, it's time to start adding soil. This comes about each time you add something that can be used in the novel. This can include characters, worldbuilding, plot events you think will be cool, or random pictures that make you experience specific emotions.

Anything and everything you collect to write your novel goes into that planter box, and forms your first layer of soil.

Sometimes I'll watch Netflix and will realize that I'd love to have a character similar to the one I'm watching, but they'll have a twist or have some additional characteristic. I take a minute to jot down the idea and stuff it into a Scrivener document.

Perhaps I happen across a documentary about ancient Egypt and the flooding of the Nile, and decide to use that in a book about plotting. In goes another metaphorical handful of soil. In my case, this is a document, but maybe in yours it's an index card.

A river gradually deposits rocks and sediment. We gradually accrete characters, concepts, and cool scene ideas. This is our fertile ground, and when we create the outline it will draw from everything we've added.

This research phase is a lot of fun, and I tend to add little bits to several projects at once. As of this writing, I'm currently plot gardening *The Ark War*, *The Dark Lord Bert*, *War Mage*, and *Dryker's Folly*. Each has its own Scrivener document, all available both on my phone and tablet so I can add notes whenever a thought occurs to me.

War Mage and *Dryker's Folly* both have about 7,000 words written. That number isn't coincidental, as it happens to be my daily quota. Both books received one full day of discovery writing, because I find that writing the first few chapters tend to really accelerate the plot gardening. I think of this process as sprinkling the first few seeds.

Then I set both books aside and started working on this book. My subconscious is happily fertilizing the planter boxes, and I've added a bunch of notes to each book even though I'm not actively writing either. The characters are getting deeper, and developing their own problems. Conflict between them is naturally arising, which in turn is shaping the plot.

We're going to be using this method throughout the book, and it's why the first exercise is setting up your planter box. Once you've got that, your subconscious will eagerly begin filling it.

How to Plot Your Novel Videos

Throughout this book you're going to hear a lot about a little goblin named Bert. Bert is a character in my novel, *The Dark Lord Bert*, and I've documented every stage of his creative evolution in a video format.

You can view the series on my YouTube channel at youtube.com/chrisfoxwrites. There are also videos on productivity, motivation, craft, and marketing. I keep them all ad free, as a sort of repository for the writing community.

They're meant to be supplementary to this book, and give you a way to see the process in action. If anything in the following chapters isn't clear, give the videos a look and see if they help clear anything up. If not, shoot me an email at chris@chrisfoxwrites.com and feel free to ask. My inbox is a busy place, but I will try to answer everyone.

A Note About Exercises

If you've read the previous books in this series, you're already familiar with the exercise portion of each chapter. If not, here's the deal. No matter how much you read about something it is not the same as actually doing.

This book is designed to teach practical principles, and the exercises offer a very simple way to apply them. So please, please, please do the exercises. If not, I will totally call your mother and tell her.

That said, if you are one of the people who likes to read a book like this in one sitting, then I've gathered the exercises into a single chapter at the end of the book. If you want to do them after you finish reading that's completely fine. So long as you do them.

Exercise #1- Set Up a Planter Box

Before we can start gardening, we need a place to garden. You need to pick a way to organize your novel, be it Scrivener (which I use), Evernote, Word, Ulysses, or anything else that works for you. Whatever you pick, know that organization is key. You want separate boxes for the following:

- Scenes / Chapters
- Characters
- Locations
- Research

Some authors prefer more, and some less. Experiment until you find which works for you. I'm still adjusting my process and the more I do it, the more efficient I've become.

Bonus: Go watch the first *How To Plot Your Novel From Scratch* video located at youtube.com/chrisfoxwrites. There are a total of five videos, and they're about 7 minutes each.

2

ADDING SOIL

Now that we've set up our first planter box, it's time to add a layer of soil, metaphorically speaking. This begins by defining the kind of book we're writing. Gardeners need to know what kind of plants they are tending. Tomatoes have very different needs than corn, or roses. The right amount of water, sun, and the season they're planted in all vary.

What kind of book are you writing? Is this a steamy thriller? Or dark horror? Maybe you want to do a space western. You may not even know that much to start, and that's okay. Simply asking the question will start your brain working on solutions.

In my case, I decided I wanted to write a tongue-in-cheek comedy where everyone in the world embodied a single trope. For those not familiar, I highly recommend checking out TvTropes.org, which provides access to tens of thousands of these bite-sized cliches.

Anyway, I figured I could have tropes like the hero, or the dark lord, or the farm boy, or the 'well, actually...' kid.

All I really knew was that I wanted the tone to be funny, and that's enough to start.

Then I started defining the basics of the story using something I call the LAYER system.

The LAYER System

- Lead
- Antagonist
- Yard
- Engagement Point
- The Return

Every story begins with a great character. The two most important are the Lead and the Antagonist. Our lead is the star of the story. They're the person with the most page time, and the most to lose.

We don't need to know much about them yet. A vague idea is plenty. *The Dark Lord Bert* was originally called *The World of Cliche*. I decided that I needed the most cliche person possible, and I created a moisture farmer as a tongue-in-cheek ripoff of Luke Skywalker from Star Wars.

Next I worked on my antagonist, who is just as important to the story as the lead. This is the person, force, or thing that will oppose the lead you've just created. In my case, the first draft was a dark lord named JRPG (Japanese Roleplaying Game). He's been powered up by his dark lord trope, but I had no idea what that really meant. Still, it was enough to get my subconscious chewing on the problem.

Once I had a lead and an antagonist I started to define my Yard. Your Yard encompasses both setting and all the worldbuilding we'll be doing throughout this book. Everything you create to define setting—every character, every custom, and every idea—lives somewhere in that metaphorical yard.

The first thing I added to mine was the idea that tropes could be implanted into a socket in each character's chest. Whenever a character changed their trope, it would alter their personality, skills, and abilities. The more rare the trope, the more powerful the abilities, and the more pronounced the drawbacks of the trope.

You want to come up with the same kind of material for your story. What makes your novel unique? What's the premise? What is the world like? The culture? Your yard encompasses all of that. Right now, though, it's a barren field, waiting for you to plow it.

Where does your novel take place? Are you writing a Florida action adventure book? Is it set in space? Some historical setting? You get to decide, but defining it early is important. It can be vague to start, but we need to at least have some idea where and when our novel takes place.

Start with the location, time, or if Fantasy / SF (Science Fiction), what fictional location it's set in. Knowing these basics will begin fertilizing that planter box.

Once we've started tilling our yard, we're ready to start on the story itself. Every story has a beginning and an ending. Your Engagement Point represents the beginning. Where is your character when the novel begins? What is their ordinary world like? This is your chance to define it.

In my case, I decided my moisture farmer would live on a farm with his family. That's it. I didn't have anything else to go on, but I also didn't need it yet, as you'll see later. This Engagement Point ended up being completely different, but defining the first version gave me something to work with, and that's all we need.

Lastly, I needed to define an epic ending. This is called the Return, based on Joseph Campbell's Hero's Journey, which you'll see referenced often throughout this book.

What will the final confrontation between the lead and the antagonist look like? Does your lead need to run into an airport and vault the security checkpoint so they can stop their love from boarding a plane? Are your lead and antagonist locked into a duel to the death with laser swords?

Come up with a cool ending. This will probably change, possibly several times. Just come up with a vague idea.

Once you've done all the above, you should end up with something like this:

Lead- a bored moisture farmer wishing for a life of adventure.

Antagonist- an evil dark lord who embodies the most amusing tropes from video games like Final Fantasy.

Yard- set in the World of Cliche, where everyone has a trope that defines their personality and abilities.

Engagement Point- the lead is living on a moisture farm with his family, and badly wants to join the resistance to help fight the evil dark lord JRPG.

Return- our lead and antagonist will meet in an epic fight. The lead will beat the dark lord, and take the trope for himself (sequel!).

Notice that each step is really short and vague. I don't

even have names for the characters. All I have is a simple concept, really. But that's exactly what we're after. We need a starting point, and this is how we get it.

Now I realize that we've blasted through the LAYER technique, and that this chapter is short. That's by design. I want you to start thinking about your story, and the rest of the book is going to build on the premise you create below.

~

Exercise #2- Add Some Soil

Create a document in your Planter Box and use the LAYER technique to generate the first layer of soil. This first version should only be a few paragraphs long, as my example was. If you're inspired to make it longer, though, don't censor yourself.

Bonus: Spend some extra time fleshing out your Yard. What is your world like? Are there powers or abilities? If this is a detective story, what sets it apart from other detective stories? Brainstorm three unique concepts, places, inventions, or characters and add those documents to your planter box.

PART II

YOUR GARDENING TOOLS

3

THE BASICS OF STORYTELLING

E very gardener needs to know as much as they can about their climate, their soil, the plants they are growing, and any local pests that could be a threat. In that same way we need to understand the basics of storytelling. It helps me to think of these basics like tools. Gardeners have rakes, shovels and trowels. We have Beats, Pacing, and Story Conflict.

This chapter will help you add the first tools to your shed, so you can properly tend to your garden. We're going to cover **Setups & Payoffs, Story Conflict, Beats & Pacing**, and choosing your **Point of View Characters**. Collectively these skills are going to help us craft the flow of the novel.

Each section is designed to be basic, but I'd encourage you to look for other books on these topics. These are the formative skills that will help you achieve mastery. What you'll find here is only the most basic level, but it will establish the language we're using for the rest of the book.

Before we get into the meat, though, I want to talk for a moment about the concept of scenes. I use these instead of chapters, because different genres have different length requirements. In epic fantasy you might have four or five scenes in a single chapter, whereas in my own fiction I always do a single scene to a chapter.

Chapters are freeform and based on genre. Scenes are a more fluid way to talk about segments of story, so that's what we'll be using.

Setups & Payoffs

The easiest way to break down the idea of a novel is into a series of setups, followed by corresponding payoffs. Every scene in your novel will contain one or more of these setups or payoffs. The closer that scene is to the beginning of the book, the more likely you'll see a setup. The scenes at the end are laden with payoffs.

Drawing on my premise from the last chapter, if I want a big confrontation between my moisture farmer and the dark lord, then I have to set that up. I envisioned what this fight would look like, and then considered all the events leading up to it. I had to work my way backward, and look for places where I could plant the right seeds.

> For Farmer to be strong enough to oppose Dark Lord, he must go on some sort of quest, and he has to succeed.

> For Farmer to go on a quest, he needs a reason to leave his moisture farm.

I started thinking about that scene. How or why would Farmer leave his farm, and how could I set that up in a way that fit the humorous tone of the book?

Think of every setup or payoff as a dot, and you're going to write scenes that connect all those dots. If the ultimate

payoff is that Farmer has to become a true warrior ready to defend his world from the dark lord, then I need to **setup** someone with room to grow into that warrior.

By making him a distracted farm boy, I define his character arc. Farmer will go from ordinary to hero, and I'll get him there by setting it all up, and then delivering the payoff.

For me, figuring out payoffs usually come first, and then I work back to setups. If I need the hero to fire a gun at the end of the book, then I plant that gun in the first or second act. People need to understand that weapon exists, so when the hero is presented with a dilemma they'll say, "Oh, I bet he'll use that gun / power / informant I saw in the first act."

If things are not properly setup, readers will cry foul. We'll feel cheated. If you remember just one thing from this book, **always setup your payoffs, and payoff your setups.** Readers will thank you. If you don't, you'll leave dangling plot threads, and nothing drives readers nuts more than setups that don't deliver, or payoffs they couldn't predict because they weren't set up.

Conflict

We've been told our entire author lives that conflict is the heart of stories, and it is. But conflict by itself is meaningless. Having two characters fight is conflict, but if that conflict has no plot purpose your readers will check out and find something else to read.

They have to care. They have to have a stake in the outcome, which they gain by seeing the stakes through the eyes of your point of view characters. As the stakes rise, and our hero has to confront obstacles, conflict arises naturally.

This conflict is divided into two types, external and internal. These typically manifest in one of four forms taught globally at high schools and early university, along with words like theme.

- Man versus Man (External)
- Man versus Nature (External)
- Man versus Society (External)
- Man versus Self (Internal)

Man versus Man represents the vast majority of commercial fiction, so much so that I'm not going to spend much time on the other three. Most of the examples in this book will focus on that style of conflict, because that's the kind that, in my experience, sells books.

We create conflict by ramping up the stakes between the protagonist and the antagonist. As the author, you need to show your reader what the protagonist will lose if she fails. What's on the line?

Then, you need to show the forces arrayed against her. What will she have to overcome to achieve her goal? Only once these two factors are established will any conflict matter. Story conflict arises from the protagonist struggling to achieve their goal, while being opposed by the antagonist or antagonists.

Put simply, the hero wants something really badly, and their whole world will be wrecked if they don't get it. If the reader is invested in the stakes, they'll binge read until 2 am. The harder the character struggles to get what she wants, the more invested they will be.

Put your character's back to the wall in whatever way you can. Raise the stakes. Is your character going to lose their job if they stand up for their principles? Then maybe their mortgage is already a payment behind, and losing this job will cost them their family's home.

Then ramp it up again. What if the protagonist's wife is sick? She needs medical care, which requires money they don't have. Now the character's back is up against the wall in a big way, and we get to see what she will do to fight for what she loves. Does she stick to her moral principles, or compromise them for the sake of her family?

Conflict can and should arise from all of your character's flaws. We'll talk more about those in chapter 6, but the quick version is that characters can have moral, psychological, or physical flaws.

Physical conflict is the kind we are most familiar with in action movies.

Moral conflict arises from a character being faced with a choice that will cause them to confront their own internal limitations. How far is too far, and are they strong enough to avoid temptation?

Psychological conflict is the kind of emotional turbulence that arises out of our own self. It arises from facing our phobias and insecurities, and ultimately triumphing over them.

The best stories mix all three types of conflict. If one or more types are lacking, you're lowering the possible sources of conflict, and thus lowering the overall level of tension. Tension, the understanding of the stakes if the hero loses, builds from the combination of all types of conflict. A mix of the right kinds will keep readers glued to their chairs.

Beats & Pacing

Stories are typically laid out in scenes, and each scene has one or more emotional beats. The term beats come from cinema, but has migrated into nearly every type of storytelling. Beats are, quite simply, self-contained nuggets of story with a single emotional resonance. A chapter with three beats might have a happy beat, then an anxious beat, followed by a terrified beat.

I tend to use only one beat per chapter, but many authors have long chapters with multiple beats. Both versions are viable. Either way, beats come in one of two flavors. Action beats, where something is happening to move the plot forward, and reaction beats, where the protagonist has a moment to catch their breath.

If you've got a tense, exciting scene you're looking at an action beat. If your protagonist is moping because the love interest just rejected them, that's a reaction beat. They're processing what happened to them, and then moving back into an action beat to try again.

Your job as a storyteller is to use these beats to gradually ramp up tension throughout the novel. This is done by continuously raising the stakes, and in most genres the action beats will outnumber the reaction beats.

Collectively, how you use these beats is known as pacing. A story's pacing will vary from genre to genre, but well, why? If tension is good, why not just string together endless action beats?

Because if you do you've just made a Michael Bay movie. Nothing but three hours of explosions and running, with no time to slow down and get to know our characters.

For conflict to matter, we have to care about those characters. We begin to care when we get reactive moments where we can see how the struggle is impacting this person. We watch them deal with crisis after crisis, and then pause to figure out how they're going to deal with it all.

If we spend too much time navel gazing and considering, then readers get bored. Too little, and they don't care about our characters. Different genres require differing amounts of each type of beat.

Choosing Point of View (PoV) Characters

One of the most difficult decisions for a new writer to make is deciding which point of view to use in a given scene. How many points of view should we have? And whose should we use?

The simple rule is to use as few PoVs as you can get away with. Every time we ask a reader to switch there's a cost, and a chance they won't connect with the new character they were just dumped into. I try to limit my books to no more than three protagonists and one antagonist. In practice this is harder than it sounds and I break my own rule all the time.

I don't want too many PoVs, but I do want enough to tell the story from the right perspectives. Which are those, though? How do you know which characters should be experiencing a given scene?

My rule of thumb is simple, taught to me by my first writing coach, Alida Winternheimer. **The PoV character should be the one with the most to lose in a given scene.** Ask yourself what's on the line for each character, and consider their emotional states.

Every chapter in your book should ramp up tension in some way, and that's achieved by being in the head of the person with everything on the line.

The exception to this rule is the antagonist. If showing chapters from the PoV of the antagonist the goal is to make the situation worse for the protagonist(s). We want to see the antagonist launching a daring raid, or sexting the love interest. We do not want to see them doing laundry.

Everything the antagonist does *could* fail, but they don't. Instead, the protagonist's situation is worse and our antagonist is stronger.

~

Exercise #3- Setup Your Payoffs

Take a look at your Return from the last chapter. What elements need to be properly setup? Create a chapter placeholder document for the ultimate payoff, and then one for each setup you brainstorm.

Pick a point of view for each of these scenes. Who might have the most to lose, and why? Do you need scenes from your antagonist's PoV? Create appropriate chapter placeholders in your planter box.

Bonus: Brainstorm three reaction scenes to sprinkle around the chapters you've already created. If your character experiences a setback, how does that impact them? They just got rejected by their love interest, or they discovered a clue to the murder. How do they react? What do they decide to do to further pursue their goal?

4

EMOTIONAL RESONANCE

The previous two chapters added our first layer of soil and our first gardening tools. Before we can start some serious plot gardening, though, we need to add a few more.

In storytelling, your goal is to control the emotional responses of your audience. You want them to feel a certain way, which you do by infusing beats with different emotional resonances. One beat might make someone tense, then the next deepens to real fear. Then we get a jump scare, followed by a laugh. This cliche doesn't work well anymore, but you can see what it's going for. Ideally, you take your audience through a gamut of desired emotions.

The reason why most people love *Star Wars* is that it chose its emotional resonance very well. Likewise, Netflix shows like *Stranger Things* extend great storytelling by slowly deepening our attachment to the characters, and they do this through emotional resonance. If we experience fear and hope and love alongside these characters, then we come to care for them as we do the people in real life.

This is a process that we as a species have perfected over hundreds of millennia. Storytelling has become an intricate part of our species, and understanding how it has shaped us teaches us to do the same thing with our own stories.

The Power of Myth

Brace yourselves, because I'm about to get science-y.

Humans are, at our heart, a tribal species. We form into small groups, and in ancient times the confines of those groups tended to break down when they got larger than about one hundred and fifty people. Our ancestors' tribe would splinter, and offshoots would leave to start their own tribes.

So far as we can tell, this process went on for something like two hundred millennia. We slowly spread out to cover the globe, succeeding where many rival species failed. The Neanderthal, our most recent relative and closest cousin, gradually diminished until they disappeared entirely.

Why did Homo Sapiens succeed where they, and other sub-species failed? Many anthropologists and scholars theorize that the answer is myth. Joseph Campbell spent his entire life studying the subject, because he believed it was integral to human existence.

What he found is profound. Human society might be capped around one hundred and fifty people, but only until you introduced mythology. Somewhere along the way, Homo Sapiens learned to tell stories, something other sub-species lacked. These stories contained kernels of information about our lives, about our moralities, and about our very nature. For the first time, we were able to store information and pass that information along to future generations.

Instead of every generation needing to learn about a specific predator, or about the danger of long term drought or fire, you had stories about ancient gods preparing for the great desolation, or a wicked child whose hut burned down. Each new generation could benefit from all the previous generations, an advantage we alone possessed. The parables their ancestors told gave them the basic cultural building blocks necessary to grow their society. It also provided neighboring tribes with a shared cultural heritage.

Every culture in the world developed their own myths, and there are surprising similarities between them. Each encapsulates a bit of what it means to be human, colored by the perceptions of the society that gave it birth.

Most of us are familiar with Aesop's fables. They were written nearly three thousand years ago, but the simple parables still ring true today. The idea of sour grapes is something we can all understand. Envy is a simple emotion, and one we all feel, regardless of where we were born or what language we speak. The short tale about a crow and a fox has conveyed that information in many different languages across the globe.

Myth is part of what it means to be human. Without it there would be no cities. There would be no internet. There would be no moon landing. If I ask you what the internet is, you'll recite the myth of the internet, or your version of it anyway. If I ask someone on the other side of the globe, they'll give their own, very similar myth.

Most of us have no idea how the internet works. We only know that it does. You don't need to understand the TCP-IP protocol, or understand binary to know how to use it. You only need to accept the story that society tells us. At some point someone told you about the internet, and then you experienced it, and then you told other people about it.

Effectively, myth is like a game of telephone with our earliest ancestors. And we, the storytellers, are the people passing the message to all future generations. Myth extends beyond simple story. It encompasses everything we collectively believe into one shared, racial consciousness.

When you drive down the road, you believe that people coming the opposite way will stay on their side of the line. When you go to a movie theater, you assume that people should be quiet, and those who aren't are considered rude. That shared social expectation is based on a common story told nearly everywhere. We all have shared beliefs about society, and those rise from the stories we tell.

They come from the movies, books, and plays that everyone has seen or read. If someone from India, someone from the Congo, someone from Switzerland, and someone from Argentina all watched *The Matrix*, then they'd all understand the references to the red pill and the blue pill, in the same way most people globally can tell you the story of *Romeo and Juliet*.

What does a woman wearing a ring on the fourth finger of her left hand mean? We all know the answer, because Hollywood has given us movies for decades showing that particular marriage custom.

Many people dismiss stories as simple entertainment, but that couldn't be further from the truth. Every story is designed to encapsulate a tiny slice of what it means to be human, and the more we succeed at this the more our work will impact readers.

The difference between a good story and a great one is often how well we handle character transformation.

Transformation

All humans possess an instinctual need to improve. We all know we should go to the gym. We should go for that promotion at work. We should ask them out. We should mow the lawn.

But we don't. We procrastinate, and we feel bad about ourselves.

Enter our story heroes. It turns out we don't need to mow the lawn, or go to the gym. Instead, we can take a seat in the back of someone's head and watch them do all the things we wish we had the discipline and motivation to do ourselves.

Every story begins with a character. Myth with a capital M starts with a character who needs to change. A flawed character, who has the same kind of goals and aspirations we all do.

Through the course of the story, this person will face their inner demons, and they will triumph. They will act, and overcome dire obstacles. This process will transform them from their weak current selves into a hero of epic proportions, into exactly the kind of hero we all secretly wish we were.

The really interesting thing is that it kind of works. You may have heard the saying that we're each the product of our five closest friends. We tend to mirror the people around us. Well, if the people around you are the characters in your favorite stories then you'll tend to become more like them.

Seeing someone else's transformation forces us to change a little bit too, and their journeys carry us into our own subconscious in a way that sweeps out the cobwebs now and again.

Make Them Feel

I don't know about you, but I was the lonely quiet kid who lurked in forgotten corners with my nose buried in a book. I read constantly, to the point where the only effective punishment my parents found was taking away my books.

If you'd asked me back then, I couldn't have told you why I loved it so much. Today I can. Reading those books made me *feel*. We all have different emotional gaps. There are areas that aren't being met in our personal lives.

Some readers are after romance. They want to be swept off their feet. Some readers want to solve a fun mystery. Some want adventure, in strange locales. Each of these stories fills those emotional gaps.

Eight-year-old Chris felt scared and alone a lot of the time. When I read those books I felt like I belonged. Suddenly I was strong enough to fight back. I mattered, because the characters I read about mattered.

Harry Potter really hit home for me, even though I didn't discover the series until my early twenties. Had I read it as a 10 year old I'm sure it would have been even more formative for me. It filled all of my emotional gaps. Harry came from a broken home, like many of us.

But suddenly Harry was being brought to a better life. A life of adventure, and magic, and most importantly— friends. The real message, the real emotional take away for most kids, is that they get to be popular right alongside Harry. They matter. They belong.

In the fantasy series the *Dragonlance Chronicles*, one of the main characters is a frail mage named Raistlin. Raistlin is bullied and mocked by everyone around him, but by the end of the series he literally becomes a god. I got a paper route just so I could afford enough money to binge my way through those books because the local library didn't have them.

Re-reading the books today, I can see the emotional resonance flow from chapter to chapter. I understand exactly what Margaret Weiss and Tracy Hickman were doing, and why it worked.

If you want your stories to stand the test of time, then you need to make your reader feel.

~

Exercise #4- Make Them Feel

Go through each of the scene placeholders you've created, and pick an emotional resonance. Is the scene going to make the reader feel frustrated? Sad? Angry? Amused? Remember when we said that each beat is defined by its emotional resonance?

It's time to add those definitions to the scenes you've created. When you're done you should have something like this. These are chapter names from *The Dark Lord Bert*.

- Typical Adventurers (Action, Amusement)
- Paradise (Reaction, Curious)
- The Attack (Action, Outrage)
- Boberton (Reaction, Resolve)

Bonus: It's time to use your Pacing tool. Lay your scenes out chronologically, and review the emotions you've added. If you want to build up to an incredible climax, you're going to need a number of scenes to ramp up the tension. Define three new scenes and fit them into the plot to help you do this.

If it's unclear which scenes you should add, ask yourself how you can make the situation worse. Always make it worse, so that in the end you can make it better. Setups and payoffs.

PART III

PLANTING SEEDS

5

THE FOUR PILLARS OF GREAT CHARACTERS

W e've got our planter box, our soil, and some of the tools we'll need to work our garden. Before we can go any further, though, we need to start sprinkling in seeds. The first type is character seeds, but for these seeds to sprout we need to understand how to tend them.

The mistake I made for the longest time was separating character from story. I used to worship at the three-act structure altar, and then I'd try to somehow tie in a character arc because characters are sposed to grow, right? I think I heard that somewhere once.

It wasn't until I happened on Dan Harmon's Story Circle that I realized character and plot are one and the same. The plot can and should be inseparable from the characters, both protagonist and antagonist. But we'll get there in Chapter II.

For now, let's look at what makes characters work. There are four vital qualities, and if you get all of them right, people will love your characters. They must be

sympathetic, they must **grow**, they must be **active**, and we must understand their **motivation**.

What Makes a Character Sympathetic?

You can't go very far in any book on craft without hearing the term sympathetic character. It means, quite simply, that your protagonist should make decisions as most readers would make them, given the same information you've provided.

It doesn't at all mean your character has to be nice, though that certainly helps for your protagonist. Some of my favorite chapters are antagonists doing terrible things, while I struggle to make them sympathetic. The horrified reader understands what the antagonist is doing and why. That antagonist is sympathetic.

If characters act in weird ways people disengage from the story, because they can't predict what that character will do. One of my favorite series is the *Wheel of Time*, and the protagonist begins as a very sympathetic young farm boy. By the middle of the series he's slowly going insane, and begins to act erratically.

Not surprisingly, many, many readers drop the series by book seven. They no longer understand what several of the main protagonists are doing, or why. It's *vital* that your reader understand the character, even if they don't at all like them.

Game of Thrones fans love to hate ruthless Queen Cersei, but we all understand exactly what she's capable of. She's brutal, efficient, and will do anything to protect her family. If Cersei suddenly woke up nice and decided to work with her enemies to support the common good readers would call foul. That's against her nature, and because she's made sympathetic we understand how she thinks.

We expect her to screw over everyone when it will most benefit her. If that were to suddenly change we simply wouldn't buy it.

Saving the Cat

Blake Snyder's famous book *Save the Cat* teaches us to make our protagonists likable. This isn't the same thing as sympathetic, but it's still important.

My novel *Hero Born* is based on my life as a software engineer in San Francisco. Beta readers complained that they weren't connecting with the protagonist. The plot was interesting, but they just weren't engaging. Fortunately, one of the beta readers suggested that I needed to do something to make the readers like my protagonist.

In the book, he's developing super powers and doesn't know why. I added a new intro where he uses his powers unconsciously to save a woman in a crosswalk. It was a short beat, but it showed that when he needed to act, he could. That fulfilled the second part of our requirements (active characters), and it also showed that David had compassion.

That single addition changed people's view of my protagonist, because their first impression of him was a positive one. We are a tribal species. We want to know our place in the tribe, and we're experts at labeling everything and everyone around us.

When we read we're subconsciously, or sometimes consciously, building a profile for every character, especially the protagonist. Interestingly, there is no discernible difference between the brain scan of someone thinking about a real life friend, and someone thinking about their favorite character. Both are equally real.

We've all heard how important first impressions are, and that's even more true in fiction. Is the reader going to want to spend the next four hundred pages in their shoes? Only if they're likable. A great way of doing that early is by having them, metaphorically, 'save the cat'.

Give it a shot. This tool dramatically improves characters.

Active Characters. Whoah (In a Keanu Reeves voice)

In *The Matrix*, we're introduced to Neo as a disengaged slacker leading the kind of double life we all wish we were living. And really, aren't all of us disengaged slackers, or were at some point? Remember that job that you only sort of hated? The one that was just a paycheck?

Neo is that version of you. He is easy to empathize with, because in part, he *is* you. When Neo is offered the choice between the red pill and the blue pill, you are also offered that choice. The vast majority of us take the blue pill in our real lives.

We took the safe path. Safe jobs. But we always wanted to take the red pill. We wanted to start our own business, or take that job down in the city. But we never took the risk. We were afraid to see how deep the rabbit hole went.

Almost everyone takes the blue pill, and almost everyone wonders what it would have been like to take the red. To gamble your future on a dream. Normally we can't answer that question, which means living the rest of our lives wondering what we missed out on. But suddenly you have Neo, someone we can all sympathize with, taking the risk we ourselves are terrified of.

He takes the red pill. He takes action. When Morpheus is being held by agents, Neo risks everything to go back into the Matrix and save his mentor. We admire him for that, because we all want to believe we'd do the same thing in the same circumstances.

Growth

Growth is fundamental to being human. If we're not growing, then we begin to feel stagnant. It's human nature. As an author, if your last book was a smash success it won't be very long before you start to feel restless. You have to top that big success, or at least match it.

Honestly, I believe that's why most people read. We sense that we *should* be growing and learning and doing, but that involves a lot of very painful work. Instead, we can satisfy that need through someone else's growing, learning, and doing. It's way easier to read about someone else's pain and effort than to generate our own.

Going back to *Game of Thrones*, Jaime Lannister is a despicable person that we absolutely loathe in the first book. By the fifth book he's considered by many to be one of the best protagonists. Jaime started very active, by pushing Bran out a window to protect his sister's secret. But he's selfish, arrogant, and dismissive of everyone outside his immediate family.

This makes him a terrible character we obviously dislike, but that's only the starting point on his character arc. The rest of the series keeps him sympathetic, it shows him active, and most importantly it shows that he is capable of growth and change.

Jaime's feelings for Brienne of Tarth are something he himself can't seem to accept. He cares for her, and wants her to succeed. He respects her martially, in a way he's never respected a woman before. We see his prejudice fading, and we want him to become a good person.

Then Jaime loses his hand (yeah, spoilers, I know). Not just any hand, either. His sword hand. The hand that has defined his entire identity since he was old enough to pick up a blade.

Suddenly Jaime must learn how to survive without his martial skills. He must overcome his physical disability, while also learning to do the right thing for the kingdom, and for the people, rather than for his own comfort.

We may not like Jaime, but we *get* him, and by the end we're rooting for him to become a genuinely good person. We're rooting for him to grow.

Motivation

Motivation is central to story. Without motivation, both from antagonists and protagonists, we cannot have conflict. Villain wants something. Hero wants the opposite. Someone has to win, and someone has to lose.

But it goes deeper than that. If you remove the conflict and simply look at your character's motivation, you'll find the core of story. Your character wants something they don't currently have. Obtaining that thing is going to transform them, and we're going to get to ride shotgun through the whole experience.

Remember our need to grow? Most people are not highly motivated. Not to the point where we'll give up sleep to accomplish things. Not to the point where we'll work fourteen hours a day to obtain their goals.

But we wish we were.

We wish we were willing to go the extra mile. We wish

that we cared about things with the impossible intensity that our heroes can muster.

Somehow, though, our lives have become too practical for that sort of motivation. We don't live our dreams, and instead shelve them in favor of life's harsh realities. Killing your dreams is an insidious kind of pain, but one way to combat that pain is by seeing other people live their dreams.

Not people we know, mind you. Seeing your cousin become a famous author when your dream is to do the exact same thing isn't going to combat your own fears or lack of accomplishment. It's only going to make you envious, or worse jealous.

But when you read, you become the character. That's the difference. You are that character, and you get to achieve the things that character achieves. You aren't boring house dad. You're Aranthar, Outrider of the Last Dragonflight, and by the gods you will stop Nebiat, no matter the cost.

By giving your character a powerful motivation, you convince the reader to adopt the same motivation. They want the same things our hero does, or they should anyway. The stakes, and the conflict, become very real. Real enough to stay up until dawn to see the conclusion.

Motivation is how you get readers invested in your story. We badly want Luke to somehow stop the Death Star, even though it looks impossible. The depth of his passion is magnetic.

What happens when you do it wrong?

If you screw up one of these four pillars, then readers will sense it and disengage from your novel. I know, because I've screwed up all of them at different points.

In the *Magitech Chronicles*, my main character, Aran, was

a tabula rasa. He begins with amnesia, which made it very difficult to convey motivation. Even he didn't know what he wanted. His emotional responses were muted, and he just sort of accepted everything.

He was passive, outside of combat. And people don't like passive characters with little motivation. Normally a character wants something from the beginning of the book, but in the first act of *Tech Mage*, Aran isn't sure what to want.

He sees this war and realizes that it needs to be fought, but he was basically kidnapped and forced into service. His internal conflict is lacking, because he has no clear motivation, and because he is passive. I broke the rules and paid the price.

Unsurprisingly, when we get into book two and he becomes more active and gets a clear motivation, then fans start to love him. By that point he's sympathetic, active, has a clear motivation, and he is growing.

But I waited too long to establish all four of those things, and I paid a price in reader engagement. Most forgave the stilted beginning, but quite a few people mentioned it in reviews. Had I established an active, sympathetic character with a clear motivation right from the get go readers would have been hooked far sooner.

I've resolved not to do the same thing with future series, including *The Dark Lord Bert*. As you'll see in later chapters, this decision is how and why my protagonist went from a random moisture farmer to a little goblin.

The moisture farmer was the wrong character, because he didn't have the right motivation, and he wasn't active. I could make him grow, but readers weren't likely to stick around long enough for that to unfold.

∾

Exercise #5- Flesh Out Your Protagonist

Take a look at the paragraph you wrote about your protagonist. Are they sympathetic? Will readers understand why they are doing what they are doing? This requires you to understand your character's motivation. So define that now. Think about the rough ending of your book. Why does your character want to get there? And what's on the line if they fail?

Now brainstorm three scenes, or add to existing scenes, where your hero is moving closer to their goal. These core scenes should show the reader who your character is, and what they are made of. It should show them active.

Finally, ask yourself about your protagonist. How is she different at the end? What's changed? Did she grow? Add any setups to earlier chapters, or make new chapters for those setups.

Bonus: Add a save the cat scene early in the book. What can your character do to demonstrate their competence and compassion (assuming they have one or both).

6

LAYERING IN CHARACTER FLAWS

Y ou know that one friend on Facebook who is always posting about the amazing places they are going, and the cool adventures they're having? Their feed makes them look like some sort of super person, and we wonder what lottery they won to have a life like that.

Many new authors convey their characters in exactly that way. They design larger than life heroes, or beautiful, compassionate heroines ready to meet mister or missus right. On the surface this isn't a bad thing. We need likable characters, but there's the danger of taking that too far.

The issue ties back into myth. Stories resonate because they are about real people. Real people have flaws, though, and if you present your character as too perfect, you break reader suspension of disbelief.

In practical terms they'll label your protagonist a Mary Sue or Gary Stu, especially if your protagonist is the one solving every problem.

To combat this, we need to give our characters flaws. We need to make living, breathing people, and every last person to have drawn breath has had some sort of flaw.

During my quest to master craft I ran across a course by John Truby which discussed three categories of flaw, and I loved the concept. It presented a simple way to give your character multiple flaws without picking them out of a hat. I created a video about these flaws, and in the comments section someone suggested a fourth category, which I've added.

The purpose of these flaws is to create story conflict in your novel. Conflict is what interests readers, and the best conflict arises from the character's flaws.

The categories include:

- Moral (External / Internal)
- Psychological (Internal)
- Physical (External)
- Social (External)

Moral Flaws

A moral flaw arises when a character differs from the accepted paradigm in the setting. They are willing to say or do things differently than those around them, in a way that would make other people look down on them if they learned about it.

A cheating wife in rural Georgia in the 1950s is morally flawed. If her neighbor finds out, word could get back to her husband. If he divorced her she'd be shunned by everyone she knows.

The same cheating wife in the heart of ancient Rome might have to deal with an irked husband, but the social consequences would be much less because the moral values in that time and place are radically different.

Understanding the moral values of the culture where your characters live will help you to give them flaws that will impact them in that current setting. In the example above, making our Roman wife a cheater carries a lot less weight than her Georgian counterpart. It might not even be a flaw at all.

If, on the other hand, that same Roman wife were jealous to the point where she poisoned anyone her husband slept with, then that would be an appropriate flaw for the setting.

You want to make sure that your character has at least some moral flaw. If they don't, that character is going to feel flat, because they're too perfect. Maybe they're occasionally a bit too righteous or preachy. Maybe they're easily distracted by card games. Maybe they steal everything that isn't nailed down.

What you choose should fit the kind of book you're writing, but having at least some moral shading will make that character much more sympathetic.

Psychological Flaws

Psychological flaws represent your character's emotional baggage. They're the skeletons we keep in our closets, that we desperately hope people never discover. Common examples include alcohol or drug addiction. So much so that both are cliche in nearly every genre.

Better examples include crippling insecurities. Does your character have a desperate need to please others? Are they completely codependent on their spouse? Do they have abandonment issues? Are they always sabotaging their own success?

All of us have our own inner demons. We've all lain awake at 2 am thinking about that one school dance where we learned that we are, in fact, not as smooth as we thought. We relive our failures, and all have that whispering voice telling us that we're not good enough.

Your job is to craft a flaw that fits the character in question. To do this, it helps to understand how and where they grew up, and what those experiences shaped them into.

A returning veteran from World War II is going to have a different set of issues from one that returned from Vietnam or Iraq. When examining your character consider where they live, and what they've been through. What got them to where they are today? What kind of adversity have they faced, and what sort of toll has it taken on them emotionally?

This will allow you craft one or more psychological flaws, rather than simply slapping an ALCOHOLIC label on your character.

Physical Flaws

A physical flaw includes anything that limits a character, well, physically. If they've been paralyzed, or lost a limb or an eye, those all count. But physical flaws also include things like age. In Harry Potter the protagonist is too young to make his own decisions. He's too weak to physically confront Voldemort, because he's 10.

In Hugh Howey's *Wool*, there's a chapter where the aging mayor is walking down a flight of long stairs that leads through the silo where a fragment of humanity has survived.

We see the physical toll it takes on her, and understand that an activity most of us take for granted requires a supreme act of will on her part. Her age limits her physically.

If you're writing in any setting involving guns, swords, bombs, martial arts, sports or other forms of physical conflict, then your character's relative training can be a flaw. If they're a novice, and the antagonist is a master, then their physical flaw will prevent them from overcoming the bad guy.

Having your character begin as a master in their field can absolutely work, but more often having them weaker gives you room for growth. This is especially useful if you're writing a long series. Readers love arcs that take our fairly weak protagonist and transform them into an unstoppable hero.

Social Flaws

This category was suggested by the aforementioned YouTube comment, but I really liked the idea. Characters can be disadvantaged through no fault of their own, and these flaws don't quite fall under moral, because the character's own outlook doesn't necessarily need to change.

Social flaws represent things that other characters in the setting will look down upon. If your character is an ex-con, that's a social flaw in most settings. Likewise, if your character was an adulterer in the deep south, then that would be a social flaw (to complement the moral flaw of cheating).

A bastard child, an unemployed husband, or your average sanitation worker are all looked down upon by different segments of society. What about your character prevents them from fitting in? Are they too poor to afford trendy clothes? Do they have a promiscuous reputation in a puritan setting? Are they a commoner in a story involving nobles? Are they just flat broke and having to sit down at Christmas dinner with their three successful siblings?

Social flaws should put your characters in uncomfortable situations, through no fault of their own. They are flaws only in the sense that they affect how that character is viewed in society, but these flaws can often be corrected.

A poor person can get a job, and show up at the end in a mega trendy outfit that makes everyone jealous. A promiscuous character can be vindicated, and her rival revealed as having created the whole scandalous notion. A commoner can be knighted.

Endeavor to pick flaws that can be corrected through the story.

Different Strokes for Different Folks

I recently posted a video on my channel breaking down Rey from The Last Jedi. I find the character interesting, because she's at the center of a massive controversy. Roughly half of fans claim she's a Mary Sue, with no character arc and no flaws.

The other half argue that she does in fact have flaws, and are mystified that the other side can't see it. Insults are hurled by both camps daily. It's almost as if they're speaking a different language, and in a way...they are.

Different audiences value different flaws. For me, personally, I want a story that centers on physical flaws. I want to see the young padawan grow into a Jedi knight. I want to see her face off against Sith. I want to see her struggle physically, and slowly master the lightsaber.

Basically, I want the same type of flaws that Luke had in the original trilogy. Most of the people saying that Rey has no flaws are doing so because they believe she has no *physical* flaws. She's a great fighter right from the start, and very intuitively unlocks force powers. This part of her character development all comes very easily, and fans who resonate with physical flaws claim it's too easy.

Most of those fans (myself included) tend to gloss over Rey's psychological flaws. She suffers from crippling abandonment issues, and is desperately struggling to find her place in things. She really just wants to belong, perhaps not even with her own family, but with the friends she meets in the resistance.

Most of her arc in *The Last Jedi* is trying to understand who or what she is meant to be. Is she a Jedi? Her mentor tells her that the Jedi aren't worth being. She sees Kylo pursuing the dark side, but that doesn't feel right either. Rey struggles to decide which direction to take, and in the end realizes that her only choice is to forge her own path. There is no mentor for her.

An informal poll of my friends revealed some interesting trends. People who primarily read romance, women's fiction, cozy mysteries, or really any mystery, all liked Rey and her arc. People who read science fiction, action and adventure, or thrillers were more lukewarm.

I believe the reason has to do with which flaw they're most interested in. Each reader values different emotional resonances, and each flaw will strum a different one. Your job is to understand which your reader values, and then focus more on those flaws.

If you're writing an action and adventure novel I'd be wary about making your character too strong out of the gate. If you're writing a mystery, then make sure you spend time in your characters head, and give a bit more of the psychological.

Exercise #6- Layer in Character Flaws

Make a list of three potential flaws in each category for your character. Consider which of these flaws would impact them the most in their setting. Being a slave won't mean much if they live in a colony of slaves. It most definitely would in pre-civil war America.

Choose one flaw from each category, and layer them into the character. Consider what made your character the way they are. Why do they have these flaws?

Most importantly, consider how these flaws can be lessened or removed by the end of the book. Not every character has to deal with flaws, and in fact doing so can be disingenuous. Wolverine will always be a grumpy anti-hero. But if the flaws can be faced and then overcome, how are you planning to do it?

Add appropriate setups and payoffs to your planter box for each flaw.

Bonus: Repeat this process for the antagonist. In many ways they should be a stronger mirror of your protagonist. If we're writing a romantic comedy for example, which flaws you choose can really help you amp up the humor.

7

PRESENTING CHARACTERS

Hopefully you have a better idea of who both your protagonist and antagonist are. In this chapter we're going to deepen those characters, and start adding our supporting cast.

To do that, it's helpful to understand how to present a character to the reader without resorting to our intro scene showing a PI passed out in a puddle of whiskey as our clue that they're an alcoholic.

The good news is that this takes a surprisingly small amount of detail, but those details must be authentic. Readers must envision the character in exactly the same way they think about a person they know in real life.

That level of detail flows from your understanding of each character. When we're first plotting our novel we'll often create two-dimensional placeholders, because we ourselves don't really know those characters.

Most of my side characters begin as a name I Googled backed up by a hair color and an attractiveness on a scale of 1 to 10. That's not enough to get readers interested, or to convince them that this person is real. Saying they have blonde hair and are gorgeous isn't going to cut it.

You must convince readers that every character is a living, breathing person.

For me, the easiest way to create a character is to base them on someone I know. When I say know, though, I mean that loosely. I've never met some of the people who inspired my best characters.

I based one such character on a pretty brunette who sat across from me every day on the ferry. I never knew her name, and we never spoke to each other, but I made a game out of imagining what her life was like, and what job she was heading into the city to do.

This sort of behavior may seem stalker-y, but writers everywhere have been doing it for time immemorial. Making up stories about the people you walk by is a great way to flex your creative muscles, and can lead to some of your best characters.

In this case the important thing for the character I created was understanding mannerisms. Ferry Girl always brushed her hair back over the left ear, never the right. She sat with her legs pulled up tight against the seat, and clutched her bag tightly to her chest. She almost never looked up from her phone, and her eyes were always scanning back and forth intensely as she read.

When I unobtrusively study people I'm always looking for similar details, because its those details that readers latch onto.

I haven't given you any concrete information about Ferry Girl, but based on what I've told you I'm sure you could make some guesses about her personality and life. Those guesses may or may not be right, but the important thing to note is that all people make them. Assumptions are like air to our species. If you give the reader a few details, they'll start building entire lives without even being asked.

All it takes is a simple sketch. Readers will fill in the rest for themselves, as long as you provide something to ground the character in. Nor does that need to be visual. I work out next to someone with terrible, appallingly bad halitosis. I've moved to another machine sometimes, just to avoid the stench. That kind of detail really brings a character to life, and is something that the reader will remember every time they think about that character. Oh, that's the guy with the bad breath.

Do you know anyone who doesn't understand personal space? Or someone who never speaks loud enough for you to hear? Use that, and your reader will print out a mental label and slap it on the character. MUMBLES.

When you come right down to it we only really use 5-6 mental labels to classify most people. Cousin. Wife. Fat. Young. Tall. Timid. Rich. Arrogant. We've got a collection of these we apply to specific people, and it makes it easy to envision them. If you provide a few labels for readers, they'll consider that character just as real as anyone else they know.

Exercise #7- Plant a Few More Seeds

Consider each of the flaws you added to the protagonist in the last chapter. Envision a way to express each to the reader without ever coming right out saying what it is. Your goal is to get the reader to append the right label all on their own.

If your character has the psychological flaw TIMID, then how does that manifest? Does he avoid eye contact? Does he have the right answer to a question in class, but is too frightened to speak up when the teacher asks, thereby allowing the antagonist to answer it for him?

Repeat this for each flaw, in each category. Now take a look at your chapter placeholders. When in the story does each of these flaws need to be set up? Create placeholders for each of the chapters you've brainstormed, or add notes to existing scenes if it makes sense to reveal those flaws there.

Remember that the goal is to get the character to say, "oh, that's the clumsy girl." You never want to tell them she's clumsy. Show them by having her spill her drink, and they'll generate their own label.

Bonus: Create an ally / friend / sidekick for your protagonist. Repeat exercises #5 and #6 to define them, then repeat this exercise to decide how you will reveal their flaws and personality to the reader.

THE BASICS OF WORLDBUILDING

We only have one more tool to add to your shed before we're ready to dive into some actual gardening. This last tool is my favorite, and one I've been using since I first discovered *Dungeons & Dragons* when I was six. That tool is worldbuilding.

Some people might say setting instead of worldbuilding, but worldbuilding encompasses so much more than simple setting. Worldbuilding *includes* setting, but it also includes the wealth of secondary characters that populate your world. I separate these from 'characters', because I'm not necessarily talking about the PoV characters, or even the supporting cast they'll meet in the novel.

I'm talking about your setting's famous people and the power brokers, and anyone else who defines the political or cultural landscape. The corrupt mayor we may or may not hear about in the first book. The woman who killed the king and disappeared with his sword fifteen years ago, never to be seen again. The town whore. Every character you create, every historical war you flesh out, every neat local custom you insert is another bit of it.

We take this part of craft seriously in science fiction and fantasy, and my genre has become known for it. Living, breathing worlds are required with our stories. Our readers expect them. Not every genre has the same demands, but all can benefit from worldbuilding.

Family trees are worldbuilding. Timelines are worldbuilding. Random poetry written from the perspective of your protagonist is worldbuilding. In today's frenetic publishing world we may not feel like we have time for any of this stuff, but I'm here to present a counterargument.

The more you ground yourself in your world(s), the richer your stories become. All these little details that you dream up over time will trickle into your stories. They allow your reader to suspend disbelief, and to accept that they have entered a world as real, perhaps even more real than our own.

The greater the detail, the more invested they will be. The more invested they are, the greater your chance of doing this for a living.

So where do you start?

Back in the LAYER step, you were asked to decide what type of story you were writing. We were talking mostly about tone, but that decision also impacts the genre you choose, which in turn impacts the kind of worldbuilding you'll need to do.

Jurassic Park is about a theme park with dinosaurs. That premise, however, can fit into several different genres. The movie (and book) is a thriller, but what if it were a horror movie? It could have ended with no one making it off the island. How might that have changed the story, and the things the audience needed to be told?

It could have been a love story, or a redemption story. It could have been about sentient dinosaurs. It could even have been a comedy.

Everything you build cascades out of genre, and picking the genre before you begin worldbuilding is smart. If you're writing a horror novel, your story will have different emotional needs than if you're writing a techno-thriller. If Jurassic Park had been a horror movie, then understanding the science behind the dinosaurs might not have been as important.

It's possible the director (because it probably wouldn't have been Spielberg) could have gotten away with much less about genetics, and focused instead on people desperately trying to survive against various dinosaurs. Most horror fans would have been fine with that, and the worldbuilding around genetics may not have mattered.

As a techno-thriller it was absolutely vital that the audience understand how and why dinosaurs could be cloned. The setting is very much a part of the story, and the worldbuilding reflected that. Before his death, Michael Crichton talked a lot about Jurassic Park and its development.

Let's walk a few meters in his shoes. What if we were Crichton? Let's say we woke up with his idea for a dinosaur theme park. To write that book we'd need to answer a whole bunch of questions.

- How could dinosaurs exist?
- Where would a park be located?
- How would that park be funded?

Answering these questions would require research. Maybe we did some Googling, and / or watched some documentaries. Maybe we read a biography or two. All of that might yield the following:

- Sequencing DNA might allow us to understand how to insert snippets of code to clone dinosaurs. Alternately, the dinosaurs could be robotic, or somehow managed to survive undiscovered.
- A park would have to be remote, ideally not within United States' borders, so it wouldn't be subject to its laws.
- You'd need massive funding, more than even a single rich person could afford. That means you'd need the backing of other powerful people, which could create conflict.

Now we can actually get our hands dirty, and this is where the worldbuilding really begins. Crichton made his first big creative choice by deciding his dinosaurs would be cloned. He could have taken the *Journey to the Center of the Earth* route, and assume that dinosaurs were still alive. He could have had robot dinosaurs.

But Crichton understood that the public was fascinated by the idea of cloning and how it might affect our lives. So he decided to pursue that route instead of the others. But that also forced him to do some worldbuilding.

To clone dinosaurs we need their DNA. Crichton realized that a plausible way that might be possible would be a mosquito frozen in amber, and that became one of the cornerstones of his worldbuilding. Think about how early you're introduced to that fact in the plot.

I have no idea where Crichton was when he made this choice, but it could have been in the shower. Or daydreaming during a meeting. Or while watching *The Land Before Time*. Who knows? Worldbuilding is quite different from writing prose, because so much of it happens organically.

What you, the creator, need to do is identify the needs of your story, and then think about how that could exist. Turn on that inner five year old, who is always asking why.

Do the Research

Crichton created the fictional island of Isla Nublar near Costa Rica, a completely plausible location for his park. He did this, because he'd been to Costa Rica and knew the culture and the weather. That made it simple to create his fictional island using pieces he took from his real life experiences. That provided authenticity and makes the book, and movie, immersive. He may not have visited Costa Rica intending to do research, but that's exactly what it proved to be.

If you were writing Jurassic Park and didn't know anything about genetics, then it would be nearly impossible to write it convincingly. Any geneticist would instantly pick apart your work, and even lay people might not buy it. I'm looking at you, James Patterson's *Zoo*.

That's the antithesis of what we're after. We want to create immersion, and get our readers to suspend disbelief. I ran into this problem when I was writing *Destroyer*, my first military SF book. I didn't understand Einstein's general theory of relativity, or how faster than light travel might be possible. But readers of military science fiction all know exactly how it works, and will shred you if your FTL system doesn't make any sense. I'd seen them do it to other books, and didn't want mine to be their next victim.

So I bought an audiobook called *Einstein: His Life and Universe* that served both as a biography, and as an introduction to Einstein's work. Two weeks later I knew the basics of relativity and was able to create an interesting, semi-plausible FTL system called a Helios Gate. That concept wouldn't exist if I hadn't done the research.

As a fun aside, I learned all about Einstein, who is one of the most fascinating people in history. A little known fact? He was kind of a dick. I've used his specific brand of dickishness as the foundation for two separate characters, and both are fan favorites. Authenticity, again.

Much of your worldbuilding is dependent on you knowing the things your characters would know, and understanding the underlying rules of your world. If you're writing epic fantasy, things like magical travel, sending messages, or waging war all require you to do a great deal of worldbuilding. You need to consider what magic is capable of, and how that would influence your world.

But you'd also need to understand things like how far a horse can go in a day. Historically, where do villages tend to spring up? (Answer: Every 10 miles, because that's how far your average person walked without a car, bike, or horse.) Then, you'd need to consider your world. If everyone has access to flying horses how does that change things?

Would villages be further apart? What if there are monsters haunting the woods around each town? How would that affect things? Would they need a wall around every city?

Good worldbuilding arises from understanding what makes your world different from our own, and how those differences might change society. If your story is set in our world, that's easier to do, but still just as important.

One of the romance authors I most admire is Rosalind

James. Ros, as she's known by the legions who follow her work, sets her wonderful stories in New Zealand. She knows the country well, and her intimate knowledge bleeds into her stories.

People feel transported to New Zealand, because she's giving them all the sensory detail, the local customs, and the emotional highs that being someplace that amazing can reach. Her worldbuilding is rich and immersive. It achieves exactly what we're all hoping to do.

Worldbuilding Videos

Worldbuilding is one of my favorite things (tm). It's so much fun to create entire worlds, and has been my top hobby since elementary school. It's a vast, vast topic with a nearly infinite number of areas to study.

It's also incredibly overwhelming, and if you're feeling overwhelmed at the idea, I'd encourage you to find other resources. Worldbuilding will take time to master, but it can be pretty fun. One chapter isn't going to even scratch the surface, though I hope it's gotten you thinking about how you can deepen your own worldbuilding.

As I jumping off point, I'd recommend my video series. They're paired up with my *Magitech Chronicles*, and go into how I created the magic system, the Umbral Depths, and names, and include other useful worldbuilding techniques.

One of the next books I am likely to write, will cover this subject in much greater detail, specifically how it applies to science fiction & fantasy (SF&F). Yeah, I've got a mailing list if you want to know when that comes out. =D

In the meantime, I'm hoping this served as a quick overview of worldbuilding. You don't need to know it all right now, so long as you're starting to accrete your own world-building pieces.

Exercise #8- Adding More Soil

What makes your world unique? Do you have magic? Super technology? Or is it a cozy mystery set in an exotic location on another continent?

Generate a list of things you'll need to flesh out to bring that world to life.

If you're writing that cozy mystery, ask yourself the questions a traveler would ask. Does your exotic location have internet access? How do the locals travel? By boat? Foot? How do these things influence the local culture? What sort of character(s) might live there? What would the locals' daily concerns be? How do people earn their living?

If you're writing SF&F and have magic, or some sort of technology that doesn't exist in our world, how does that change things? What are the ramifications of this technology? How would people use it for profit? What would change if everyone had access to it? Warfare? The economy? Space travel?

Generate a list of things that will be different about the setting, and write a paragraph describing each.

Bonus: If you are an SF&F author, pick an exotic real world location and flesh out all the ordinary things about it, as described above. If you are any other type of author, create a radical magic or technology and add it to your world, even if you don't plan on using it in the novel. Consider how that might affect your characters' lives, the global economy, or how various religions might react.

What are the ramifications? Answering these questions will tell you a great deal about your world.

PART IV

ADDING GUIDE POLES

9

CHOOSING A STRUCTURE

O ur shed contains the tools we need, and we've got a nice thick layer of soil in our planter box. We've created a few character seeds, and sprinkled them in.

The next phase of your gardening will provide those characters a guide pole to grow right up alongside, just like tomatoes. That guide pole is your outline.

Before you can create it, you need to pick a structure to adhere to. I cover two in this book: the three-act structure and Dan Harmon's story circle. There are many, many other types of story structure and some genres work better using ones not covered in this book.

What they all have in common is that they contain plot points. They are the dots you need to connect, and while those dots are different in a tragedy than they are in a comedy, the principle is the same.

After reading the next two chapters, consider the needs of your genre. Do you need the character to transform? Or are they largely static from book to book. If they're mostly static, I'd suggest the three-act structure.

If they're designed to grow and change, then have a look at the story circle. In both cases, notice that the structures are driven by plot points, and that only the emphasis of those points change.

Books and Movies We'll Be Referencing

Throughout the rest of the book, we'll be using specific books and films as examples. Most of the examples are movies, since that's proven to be a more common language than books with most authors. Everything we're covering can and should also be applied to your favorite books, and I'd encourage you to re-read a few with an eye on story structure.

Anyway, here's the list:

- Star Wars A New Hope (1977)
- Dawn of the Dead (2004)
- The Matrix (1999)
- A Song of Ice & Fire / Game of Thrones (1996 - 2142?)
- Romancing the Stone (1984)
- Harry Potter (1998 - 2007)
- Cast Away (2000)

I realize I may get some eye rolls from purists, but I sincerely believe that story is story, regardless of medium. After six books for writers, I've learned how hard it is to get people to read, and if I listed all books, less than 10% of you would read even one of them. That statistic is 100% made up.

Most of you have seen at least two of the movies above, or possibly read some of the books. Those of you who haven't are far more likely to rent and watch one of these then you are to download and read a book, but if you're inspired to do both...awesome!

Guess what the exercise is?

∼

Exercise #9- Fertilize that Soil

One of the best ways to get your subconscious churning is by studying work you love. Pick the book or movie you are most familiar with in the list above and buy or borrow a copy. The idea is to take something you've already seen, and to watch or read it again with a critical eye, now understanding how story structure works.

For this exercise all you need to do is acquire the book or movie. You can watch it if you'd like, but if you do so before reading the next couple chapters, then I'd encourage you to watch it again afterwards.

Bonus: Pick something from the list you aren't familiar with and buy or borrow it.

10

THE THREE-ACT STRUCTURE

The three-act structure is so named because it possesses a beginning, middle, and end. Each portion has a corresponding act, and within each act are a collection of chapters building up to a specific plot point. We'll go through each of the acts below, and you can see what criteria are required to advance the plot from act to act.

You will sometimes hear about the four-act structure. It's less popular than the three-act structure, but very similar in nearly all respects. The primary difference is that it divides the second act in half, which makes a lot of sense if you review the plot points below.

I used the three-act structure for my first ten novels, and I have no doubt I'll use it again. Even if you think the story circle is a better fit, understanding three-act structure will help you develop a keen storytelling eye.

Structure Overview

Act One- Setup

- Meetings
- Inciting Incident
- First Gateway

Act Two- Confrontation

- The First Crisis
- The Midpoint
- The Second Crisis
- The Second Gateway

Act Three- Resolution

- The Climax
- The Resolution
- The Denouement

Act One- Setup

Act One is the setup. We're being introduced to the protagonists, usually the antagonists, and are seeing the story problem. By the time the first act ends, we'll understand what the hero has to do, and what's at stake if she fails.

When I say story problem, I mean the problem that will drive the plot forward. The protagonist is going to need or want something badly enough to risk changing in order to do / get it.

1st Plot Point- Meetings

We've heard all our lives about how important first impressions are, because it's true. Humans are profilers by nature. We use something called heuristic learning, what most people call profiling, to identify the world around us.

If we touch a hot stove and we get burned, then we'll assume that every time we see that orange glow on the burner, the burner is hot. This is very useful from a survival perspective, and makes it easy for us not to do stupid things more than once. It also means that if someone else does something stupid, we can learn from it instead of making the same mistake.

Your readers are, so far as I know, all humans. They all learn this way. When they meet a new person, they compare that person to people they already know to decide how they feel about them. This plot point is your chance to get the reader to do exactly that. You can show them that your protagonist is smart, or deadly, or gorgeous, or popular, or bipolar, or whatever quality they need to have.

The Meetings plot point shows us the protagonist's everyday life, usually doing something they're good at. We give them a small problem, and show the reader how they adeptly solve it. We do this, because all humans respect competency.

In *Star Wars*, Luke Skywalker demonstrates his knowledge of droids, "This one has a bad motivator." We understand that he's proficient at farm work, and confident in his abilities.

In *The Matrix*, Neo is selling illegal software to a group of shady people. We know he's a skilled hacker, but we also see that Trinity hacked his system. There's someone better out there, and Neo wants to find out who it is. We can see that in Neo's body language and his actions. The audience also wants to know, and follows him willingly to the next plot point.

Dawn of the Dead begins with Ana, a young overworked nurse navigating through the complex hospital bureaucracy even though her shift has already ended. She's clearly tired, but instead of leaving, Ana first takes care of the last assignment given to her by a doctor. She powers through the exhaustion in a way we can all empathize with and admire.

2nd Plot Point- The Inciting Incident

This is the first real crisis in the protagonist's life, a real interruption to their world. The inciting incident introduces us to the story problem. Now that we know who they are, we need to forcibly thrust them into their adventure.

Especially if you didn't have them do so in Meetings, this is a great place to have your protagonist save the cat. Not only will this shake up the protagonist's world, but it will show the reader that they can handle a crisis.

Luke Skywalker discovers a hologram showing a gorgeous princess in desperate need. His problem? He wants to save her.

Neo leaves his apartment and meets Trinity at a club. She tells him of the Matrix's existence, and offers tantalizing hints about it. The story problem? What is the matrix? Neo will do anything to find out.

Ana awakens to find her ten-year-old neighbor, now clearly a zombie, attacking. Her husband is badly bitten, and being a nurse, she springs into action. She locks the zombie out of their room, and tries to staunch the flow of blood (she's saving the cat). The story problem? Zombies, yo. Ana must find safety.

3rd Plot Point- The First Gateway

This plot point changes the protagonist's life forever. They can no longer return to their everyday life. They're committed, whether they like it or not. This event thrusts them firmly into Act Two, where they will have no choice but to confront the story problem, and the antagonist.

This is the moment when Luke Skywalker returns to his farm to find his aunt and uncle dead. He can't go back. He must go forward, into adventure. He must follow Obi Wan.

Neo takes the red pill and finds out exactly how deep the rabbit hole goes. He's pulled from the Matrix, and forced to confront the reality that his entire life, everyone's entire life, is lived in a virtual reality controlled by machines.

Dawn of the Dead uses a pan shot to really emphasize the first gateway, making it especially easy to spot. Ana turns in a slow circle surveying her neighborhood and realizes the horror she just witnessed in her own home is widespread, in all directions. This scene continues for several minutes and drives home how different her new world is. It concludes with her being knocked unconscious, and forcibly thrust into Act Two.

Notice how all the protagonists *cannot* go back to their previous existence. There's literally no returning to their old lives. This structure is most obvious in thrillers or fast-paced adventure flicks. It's less obvious in genres like romance, but usually still there.

> In *Romancing the Stone*, Joan arrives in Cartagena, a foreign city, mistakenly boards the wrong bus, and then falls asleep. By the time she wakes up in the middle of the Columbian mountains, it's too late to turn back.

> In *Cast Away*, the plane crashes into the ocean, and Tom Hanks must desperately struggle to survive.

This motif carries across all genres. The three-act model is one of the most common for a reason, especially in Hollywood. It carries over heavily into most genre fiction, too. You'll almost always be able to spot the first gateway.

Act Two- Confrontation

Our protagonist has been thrust into a different world, and now they have to react to this strange place. They're facing challenges, while the antagonist is gaining strength. The conflict ramps upward through nearly the entirety of this act, with only a few reaction beats for the reader to catch their breath.

When I originally learned the three-act structure, the material didn't include plot points like the first crisis, the midpoint, or the second crisis. Once I discovered those plot points my stories got a lot tighter, and plotting them became an order of magnitude easier.

4th Plot Point- The First Crisis

Somewhere about midway between the second gateway and the midpoint your protagonist is going to face a challenge. This is generally a reactive challenge, meaning they're placed in a bad situation and have to find a way out of it.

This will contrast with the second crisis, where the hero is generally proactive. They're taking the fight to their enemies. Here, the fight is coming to them.

> The Millennium Falcon is pulled aboard the Death Star, and our heroes have to find a way to disable the tractor beam. Obi Wan sets off to do that, and just after he leaves, Luke realizes that the princess is a prisoner on the Death Star. For the first time he has to make a choice, rather than rely on Obi Wan or his uncle to do it for him.

> Neo is captured by agents and interrogated. They give him a chance to cooperate, but Neo chooses to resist. During the interrogation, his mouth literally grows shut, and they implant a writhing mechanical creature inside of him.

> Ana and her new friends take shelter in a mall, but then run into three armed mall cops who disarm them and take them prisoner. Now, not only do they have to deal with zombies, but they must deal with their captors as well.

In all cases, notice that our protagonists have very little control over their situations. They aren't choosing to have these things happen, and all they can do is react and adapt as best as they are able.

5th Plot Point- The Midpoint

I've heard multiple descriptions of what the midpoint of a novel is supposed to be. Some argue that it should be a terrible crisis, and should stand in opposition to the amazing ending. I guess that works, but I lean more toward the Joseph Campbell approach.

We'll talk a lot more about the hero's journey in the next chapter, but its version of the midpoint is called *meet the goddess*. Our protagonist reaches a point where they can take a breath, and process everything that's happened to them. This usually happens alongside a goal being achieved, usually a goal that they still have from the inciting incident.

> Luke rescues Leia, something he's been wanting to do since he saw the hologram all the way back in Act One. We have a short beat where they compare notes, and then it's into the chute, flyboy.

> Neo meets the Oracle, our metaphorical goddess, and she tells him that he isn't The One. It's the exact opposite of what the audience expects, which only convinces us to further engage with the plot. What do you mean Neo isn't The One? We have to know what happens next. Neo achieves his story goal from the first act, and finally has the answers he was seeking. Or he thinks he does, anyway.

> Ana and the other survivors reach an equilibrium, and there're no more captors / prisoners. They finally achieve the safety they've been seeking since Act One, and for just a moment they can pretend that their world is normal and happy. This plot point is signified by sudden upbeat music, right after a tragic scene.

6th Plot Point- The Second Crisis

The second crisis is meant to stand in opposition to the first. Where before our hero was reacting, now they are making a choice. They are proactively securing their future.

Obi Wan is killed and Luke has a choice. He can attack Vader, or he can flee and bring the Death Star plans to the rebels.

Morpheus is captured and Neo has a choice. He can watch as they pull the plug and Morpheus dies, or he can attempt to do something no one has ever done before. He can fight agents head on and rescue his mentor.

Andy, the guy at the gun store across from the mall, is starving. Ana and our heroes resolve to save him, then flee to a nearby island where they hope they'll be safe from zombies. When the dust settles Andy is dead, and so are several other people, but our protagonists took action. They made a choice.

Notice that in each case, the protagonist pays a price. I didn't understand this in my first several novels, which is why some people complain that the story feels off, even if they can't identify why.

Our subconscious hunger for myth is only sated by someone who does the right thing, even though it costs them significantly to do so. You'll hear a lot more about that in the next chapter when we cover the Take & Pay portion of the Story Circle.

7th Plot Point- The Second Gateway

This is it. The choice that will thrust the protagonist into a final confrontation with the antagonist. They have all their allies. They've conquered their own inner demons. They've gone from reactive to proactive.

They are ready for Act Three.

Luke volunteers to fly an X-Wing in the final assault on the Death Star. He could run. He could go with Han, and fly to safety. He chooses not to. He joins the doomed rebels on their hopeless crusade to destroy the Empire's super weapon. He rises above his fears to do the impossible.

Neo starts to run from Agent Smith, instinctively. Then he slows, and turns to face Smith. He's done running away. He's ready to face his opponent. Neo charges Smith, and the two begin one of the most epic cinematic duels of all time.

Nicole steals the escape truck to rescue her dog. She's trapped, and will die without help. The camera turns to Ana and she says, "We need to do something. Now." She's become active, and is ready to go back out into the sea of zombies to save someone she now considers family.

In each case the protagonist is taking a significant risk. They're willing to confront a superior foe, and have proven that they have all the tools necessary to overcome their opponent, even if it's a long shot.

Act Three- Resolution

Act Three is the resolution of the story problem. Everything that's happened has led to the protagonist's inescapable choice. She will face her fate, and accept the consequences.

Every scene has built to this moment. We've seen that the antagonist is going to be nearly impossible to beat. Our hero has been stripped of resources, and will probably fail. But they are determined, and they are going to risk everything to achieve their goal.

8th Plot Point- The Climax

The epic battle has begun. Our protagonist wants something, and our antagonist wants the opposite. Someone has to lose and pay the price.

Luke and the beleaguered rebels assault the Death Star. They know time is running out, and that if they fail, not only will they die, but the rebellion will be extinguished once and for all. We know the stakes, and are glued to our seats as we watch the climax unfold.

Neo has beaten Agent Smith, but Smith just came back in another body, and Neo is wounded. Smith has also brought help. Neo runs, battling agents as he tries to reach the extraction point. He's able to fight them now, but it's three on one and he clearly can't win against them all.

Ana and her friends board their makeshift buses, and leave the safety of the mall. They brave a sea of zombies as they race to the docks, hoping to make it before they are overwhelmed.

9th Plot Point- The Resolution

This is the OH YEAH moment where our hero wins. The girl says yes. The hero kills the villain. Our situation is resolved, and our protagonist (usually) wins.

> Vader and his tie fighters are about to kill Luke, but Han surprises us all by returning to help his friend. Luke makes a one-in-a-million shot and blows up the Death Star. The rebellion is saved.

> Neo is shot in the chest a bunch of times. His real body flatlines. He's dead. Back in the real world Trinity whispers into his ear that he can't be dead, because she was told she'd fall in love with The One, and she's in love with him. Neo's heart starts again, and he stands back up in the Matrix. He casually destroys Agent Smith, and the other agents run. He's won.

> The mall has been breached, and Ana must flee toward the waterfront before the zombies overwhelm them. Because this is a horror movie, they pay a heavy cost and nearly everyone dies. Ana is forced to let go of people she's come to care for, and focus on her own survival. But she achieves her goal, and makes it to the boat that represents safety.

10th Plot Point- The Denouement

This plot point is optional, but if it is missing many readers will instinctually sense it. We want our happily ever after, and this is where we get to show it. The tone of the denouement varies from genre to genre, of course, but whatever promise we made in Act One needs to be delivered on here.

In a horror movie, the happily ever after is usually one person, or a few people, surviving the terrible ordeal that wiped out a lot of their friends, family, coworkers, etc.

In a romance, we get the literal happily ever after. Two people have fallen in love.

Regardless of genre though, our hero is returning to their ordinary life, but they're doing it changed by their journey.

Han and Luke are awarded medals, while Chewie gets shafted. Apparently having fur means you don't get a medal. Oh yeah, also the rebellion celebrates their survival, and hails them as heroes. Luke has realized the dream he expressed in the first act. He's helped the rebellion and has become the hero he was always meant to be.

Neo returns to the matrix, but this time as a god. He's flying around taunting agents, completely unafraid of them. Quite the opposite. Agents run from him now, and he's able to change the Matrix as he sees fit.

Ana and her few surviving friends board the boat. Michael has to stay behind, because he's been bitten. He reassures Ana that it will be all right. The last shot of the movie is him shooting himself in the head, while Ana sails to the safety she's been seeking the whole movie. Bleak, but fitting for a horror movie.

As you can see, a gory horror movie and two different SF films all follow the same template. Each uses the same emotional formula to achieve the desired emotions, and the audience is left satisfied.

That's exactly what we all strive to do, and understanding story structure can help us achieve it.

∼

Exercise #10- Add the Three-Act Structure

Create a new document in your planter box and label it Three-Act Structure. Write a short description of each plot point. They don't have to be much longer than what we created back in the LAYER step.

You don't need to make chapter placeholders yet, because you may not end up using this structure. In the next chapter we'll be creating a mirror using the story circle. Only then will you decide which you prefer.

For now, just create this single document. Give each plot point as much time and attention as it needs, and as you're doing so, always be asking questions. Do you need to add characters to the plot to make each point work? Which ones come naturally, and which have you scratching your head?

You may not be able to finish this exercise quickly, and on the first pass it's totally acceptable to put a ??? under a plot point you aren't sure how to flesh out. Do what you can, take a break, and then add to it.

Bonus: Rent one of the movies discussed in this chapter and watch it while armed with a pad of paper and something to write with. Look for each plot point and note when it occurs. Watch the setup before each plot point, and the aftermath surrounding it. Pause and rewind where necessary. Study how the movie flows from plot point to plot point. Repeat this analysis each time you watch a movie, or read a book, until it becomes second nature.

If you're not into movies pick an old favorite book and perform the same plot point analysis.

DAN HARMON'S STORY CIRCLE, PART 1

The primary difference between the story circle and the three-act structure lies in how each perceives character. You'll notice that the last chapter did sometimes mention character growth, but there are many plot points that ignore it entirely.

Character is considered separate from story, and because I grew up steeped in the three-act structure, I believed the same thing. It wasn't until I was first exposed to Campbell and his 'monomyth' that I understood the two could be woven together.

The Hero's Journey

Joseph Campbell theorized that every myth is essentially the same, and he distilled that down into something he called the monomyth. This single myth told the tale of a hero overcoming adversity to become something greater.

More importantly, Campbell believed that every human had an instinctual need for these stories. Following the hero on their own journey into the underworld requires us to metaphorically journey into our own subconscious, and doing so feeds something integral within us all.

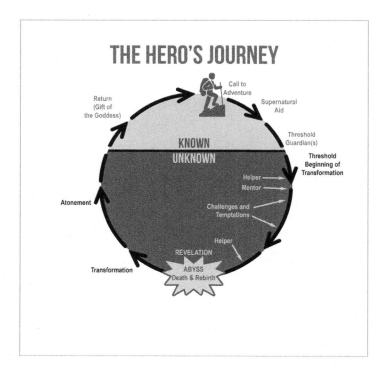

Here's the 60-second version of the Hero's Journey. The Hero's Journey begins by showing the hero's ordinary world. We see them in a normal place, doing whatever is normal for them. Their ordinary world is interrupted by the call to adventure, but at first the hero refuses the call. They want to remain in their ordinary world, because they understand subconsciously that leaving it will be painful and scary.

An external force impacts their ordinary world, and

forces them to leave it. Their village is attacked. Their MacGuffin is stolen. They learn a terrible secret. All myths are different, but Campbell believed that in this they were the same.

The character has no choice but to descend into the underworld, where they're stripped of their pride, their sins, and their weaknesses. Crossing into this special world begins the character's transformation, which will continue until the end of the story. Along the way, they are usually granted supernatural aid, a talisman, spell, or ability that will help them achieve their goals.

Campbell called this next section the Road of Trials. Our hero faces challenges and temptations that would reveal their sins and flaws, and one by one those sins would be forgiven. They need help to do this, of course, so our hero meets a mentor, and usually a helper or ally.

They reach the abyss, also called the belly of the whale. Here they meet the goddess, which took many forms depending on the culture that birthed the myth. The hero is reborn, his old self cast aside as he is transformed into the heroic form he would need to accomplish his quest.

Our hero atones for their sins and flaws, which were washed clean during their road of trials. They meet the goddess, where they are forced to make a choice. They've reached the depths of the underworld, and in order to ascend into the light they must realize that their quest is more important than their own well-being.

They seize control of their destiny, going from reactive to active, and from this point forward they are a different person. They are now ready to ascend back into the ordinary world.

To get there, they will pay a price, which often means

sacrificing the aid, mentor, or ally they were given during the road of trials. The hero is forced to want something so badly that they understand it is more important than themselves, and so they pay this price willingly, and then ascend back into the light, changed.

This is a simplistic look at a complex story form, and I highly recommend reading *Hero with a Thousand Faces*, or watching the Bill Moyers interviews with Campbell. There's an audiobook version available on Audible that is definitely worth a credit.

Dan Harmon's Story Circle

Enter Dan Harmon with his story circle. Dan is most famous for creating the show *Community*, and more recently for his smash hit *Rick & Morty*. Both are favorites of mine, largely because Harmon is so good at story structure.

About two years ago I heard he'd broken down storytelling into something he called the story circle. He gave full credit to Joseph Campbell's *Hero's Journey*, but had added his own spin to make it more accessible to modern audiences.

The result was an easy to follow formula that I used to write the novel *Tech Mage*. Unlike the three-act structure, the story circle focused on the development of my protagonist, and forced me to weave character and story together.

It's broken into eight plot points that walk through the hero's journey. They carry the hero down into the underworld, then ascend back into the ordinary world, just like they do in Joseph Campbell's version above. Before we get into the steps though, the circle itself bears some explanation.

The top half of the circle represents the hero's ordinary world. This world embodies **life, order,** and the **conscious mind.** It contrasts sharply with the bottom half of the circle, which represents **chaos, disorder,** and the **subconscious.**

Let's unpack that a little. Think of your own mind. The top half of the circle is your conscious mind. Things are orderly and well maintained here. Below, though, is a different story. That's our subconscious, and the deeper we journey into its unlit depths, the more secrets and truths about ourselves we are forced to face.

Your hero will face exactly those depths, braving their own psyche in order to become the person they need to be. Passing into this metaphorical underworld is no mean feat. It is a world of chaos and confusion.

Just as they will face their own psychological descent into the underworld, the character often faces a more literal descent where they face a series of external threats. This descent parallels their mental journey, and the deeper they get, the worse the problems they encounter on both fronts.

By the time they reach the very bottom of the circle, they

have been cleansed of their inner demons, and have faced their external threats. They metaphorically meet the goddess, where the story gives them a moment to catch their breath.

In this instant they must make a conscious choice, one that every previous trial has prepared them for. They are a new person, transformed from their old **passive** self into an **active** hero.

The moment the hero makes the choice to become active, they pass into the left half of the circle and begin their ascent back toward the light. Take a minute to consider the circle in both ways, the top versus bottom, and the right versus left. Each time your hero passes into another quadrant of the circle, they'll face major change, and by the time they return to the ordinary world, they will be the heroic version of themselves.

This next graphic gives you a look at the entire circle, complete with the plot points we'll be utilizing. We'll spend the rest of the chapter breaking down the first three.

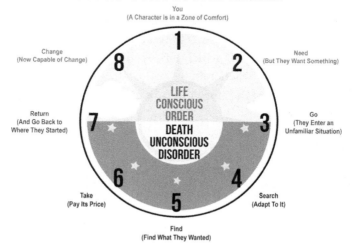

STORY STRUCTURE CIRCLE

You
(A Character is in a Zone of Comfort)

1

Change
(Now Capable of Change)

8

Need
(But They Want Something)

2

LIFE
CONSCIOUS
ORDER

Return
(And Go Back to
Where They Started)

7

DEATH
UNCONSCIOUS
DISORDER

3

Go
(They Enter an
Unfamiliar Situation)

Take
(Pay Its Price)

6

Search
(Adapt To It)

4

Find
(Find What They Wanted)

5

1- You

Every story begins with a character, and when the reader agrees to read your book, they are also agreeing to become that character. All we need to do is present them with a character, but there are two rules we must follow.

Number one, everything you tell the reader about your character here should link to their transformation throughout the book. We're already setting up the ultimate payoff.

Far more importantly, this is our opportunity to show the character's passion. We all respect people who are passionate. We find ourselves drawn to them. In this plot point you're going to show the reader just how passionate your character is, and that they are also very competent at whatever this passion is.

However, rule number two is they are real people and therefore flawed. Not randomly flawed, though. Their flaw arises from their passion. Think about Hermione Granger being a know-it-all, which arises from her passion for learning and for witchcraft.

By the end of the story, our protagonist will usually overcome this flaw.

Let's look at some examples:

Luke is an absent-minded farm boy. He doesn't care about the farm. He doesn't care about Tatooine. All he cares about is getting off that rock and joining the rebellion. He wants to be anywhere but here. Luke is the epitome of the bored teenager who has never been placed in a life-threatening situation.

We're still seeing that he's a competent mechanic, and we're told that he's a skilled pilot. But he's wasting his potential, because he's obsessed with the future, instead of making the most of the present.

At the film's climax, he will be placed in a situation where this flaw would cause him to fail, but he'll get a chance to prove that he's overcome it.

Neo is clearly a skilled hacker, as evidenced by someone willing to pay him $2,000 for a program he wrote. We see his passion for code, but we also see that he's a disengaged slacker who is willing to sell illegal software.

He takes his life for granted, and doesn't consider the consequences of his actions. By the end of the movie we need him to be a staunch leader willing to risk his life to save Morpheus. This lazy, passive version of him sets the stage for that transformation.

Ana is a hardworking nurse, and she's passionate about helping patients. But she's also too meek to stand up to the doctor who orders her around. She passively accepts his unreasonable demands, even though the audience hopes she'll stand up for herself. By the end of the movie she'll stand up to men with guns, hordes of zombies, and unwinnable situations.

This scene sets up her transformation into that hero.

2- Need

The closest corresponding plot point in the three-act structure would be the inciting incident. Our protagonist needs something. They have a problem, and they need to solve it. That problem will lead them into greater adventure, drawing them unwillingly into their ultimate transformation into a hero.

What separates this from the inciting incident is that the protagonist also typically makes a mistake prompted by their flaw. If we follow the Pixar way, this mistake is a choice between a high road and a low road.

We want Mr. Incredible to sneak out and start fighting crime, not stay home and be a boring insurance salesman. We want Luke to remove the restraining bolt.

Luke finds the recording of Leia, and hears the name Kenobi. He realizes that might be old Ben Kenobi. Luke wants to meet the hot princess, and to do that he needs to know who she is. He removes R2's restraining bolt (the mistake), because he cares more about the future than he does the present (his flaw). He takes the low road.

He's given an immediate story need. Ben Kenobi might be able to tell him more about this princess, or even go save her. We know this is what Luke most wants, but he is in his passive phase and does nothing to follow up.

Instead, he wakes up to find out that R2 straight bailed, and realizes it's his fault. If Luke can't get R2 back, his uncle will be out a lot of credits. Worse, it will mean that Luke probably has to stay on at the farm even longer. There's a lot at stake to his ordinary world.

He meets with Ben, and finally has his chance. Ben offers to take him to Alderaan. Luke refuses the call and says he has to stay here and help his Uncle. This refusal occurs to show that our protagonist is passive, so that it contrasts with their more active phase on the left side of the circle.

Neo's low road came early, back in You when he chose to go out to a club rather than get some sleep before work. He followed the white rabbit, because he badly wants answers. This arises from his passion for hacking, and we're rooting for him to take the low road.

His Need step begins when he receives a package at work after just having been chewed out by his boss. Inside is a cell phone, which rings. It's a mysterious man named Morpheus, and he tells Neo, "They're coming for you, and I don't know what they're going to do to you." Neo's scared. We're scared.

Neo gets out on the ledge of his 20th story office, but when he sees the drop he chickens out. He goes back inside. He refuses the call to adventure, and makes a terrible mistake. Just like Luke didn't go visit Ben, Neo also takes the passive route. He gets caught by the agents, because he refused to flee.

Ana is attacked by their zombie neighbor, and her husband is bitten in the throat. She has to find a way to save him, so she desperately staunches the flow of blood while trying to keep the zombie out of the room.

She fails. Ana can't protect her husband, and he dies. She's more active than Luke or Neo, but fails anyway. Unlike the others, she doesn't really have the option of refusing the call, or taking a low road. Adventure has been thrust upon her.

Her mistake is subtle, and not really a mistake at all. Ana wasn't strong enough to protect her husband. But, by the end, she will be strong enough to protect herself.

In all cases, the hero is in deep. They've got problems with no easy solution, and they've got an interest in a greater quest. They've made a mistake, but they haven't yet come to the point of no return.

3- Go

Go matches up perfectly to the first gateway from the three-act structure. In both cases, the hero's life will be forever changed by some external force. However, there is a huge difference in how that process is occurring. Act Two exists to get the hero to the ending. To fulfill the needs of the plot.

In Go, an **external force** causes the character to descend into the metaphorical underworld. They have no choice but to adapt, grow, and change to deal with their incredible situation.

They will not emerge again until they have been transformed into a hero capable of solving the story problem. Some of the most important parts of the story will take place in the underworld, and getting there should be significant in its own regard.

Luke finds his aunt and uncle dead, and his farm burned. He cannot go home. He must descend into a new, lawless world, beginning with Mos Eisley. His old life, his limitations, and his preconceptions will all be stripped away as he descends, and this scene begins that process.

Neo takes the red pill. He makes the conscious decision to see how deep the rabbit hole goes, and he enters the underworld, which in this case is the real world. He learns very quickly that the matrix was his ordinary world, and that he can never return to it now that he knows the truth. Humanity is a slave race.

Ana sprints out her front door into a chaotic world. A neighbor's house is on fire. She sees multiple car accidents. Zombies are randomly eating people. The entire world as she knew it is gone. She is now in the underworld, symbolized by the zombie apocalypse.

The only way to emerge from this underworld is to find safety, and Ana will spend the rest of the movie trying to find it.

As you can see, this step isn't that different from the first gateway, but the difference, while subtle, is very important. The protagonist is leaving their ordinary world, which is the first step of their transformation. Each step they take will move them closer to the person they need to be, but for those subsequent steps to matter we have to make this one count.

~

Exercise #11- The First Part of the Circle

Go back and read the document you created in exercise #10. Now create a new document and label it The Story Circle. Add the following:

1. You
2. Need
3. Go
4. Road of Trials
5. Meet the Goddess
6. Take & Pay
7. Return
8. Changed

Write a full paragraph for You that includes your character's passion, as well as the flaw that arises from it. Repeat this process for Need. What event is propelling your character into the story? Finally, add Go. What's the point of no return for your hero?

These descriptions should build on what you created in the previous document, and the goal is to examine your story from multiple angles to see what that jars loose in your subconscious.

Bonus: If you've got the time, re-watch or re-read the first act of the movie / book you picked in the last exercise. This time you're looking to see if it follows the story circle. What did you pick up this time that you might have missed when watching it, thinking about the three-act structure?

12

DAN HARMON'S STORY CIRCLE, PART 2

Congratulations, we've finished the first quadrant of the circle. We met a hero in You, saw them Need something, and then watched as an external force pushed them into the Go step.

Our hero has now entered the underworld. They are descending into darkness and chaos, to face their inner demons and whatever external threats the antagonist has arrayed against them.

Let's jump into the next plot point!

4- The Road of Trials

In the Road of Trials, your character must discover who they truly are. This occurs through a series of revelations, often brought about by multiple crises. Each one should touch on their flaw, and gradually teach them not only that they possess the flaw, but that it needs to be corrected in order to achieve their goals.

Everything Campbell mentioned in the Hero's Journey is accessible here. You can give your hero a mentor, which they will later lose. You can give them allies, their 'supernatural aid.' This varies from genre to genre, of course. But notice how long this section is for all involved:

> Luke and Ben have to sell their speeder, survive a seedy bar, hire a pilot, escape from the Empire, dodge chunks of Alderaan, get captured by the Death Star, and rescue the princess before the Road of Trials ends. Luke goes through a lot, and if you look at each step it requires him to do something he's never done before. He has to step up, face his fears, and become someone greater than he was back on Tatooine.

> Neo learns the terrifying truth about the matrix, and about human history. Then his training begins, and he spars with Morpheus inside the matrix. During the fight, Morpheus tells him that he is The One. One of his companions warns him that it's BS, and that he needs to run from agents like they do. Neo has reason to be afraid. He fails part of his training, which causes him to doubt further. He settles into this new life, and realizes all that he's given up. He has to eat gruel, and live in a cold, dingy ship, squatting over the ashes of a dead world.

> Neo sees and does a lot. Along the way he must shed his old identity, and go from a disengaged slacker to the kind of hero who might be able to free humanity from the machines. This transformation happens gradually, and by the time he meets the Oracle in the next section he is ready to be reborn into a hero.

> Ana reaches the mall, which offers a certain degree of safety. She and her friends are quickly overcome by CJ and his mall cops, who lock them up in one of the stores (with

no bathroom...ew). Not only does Ana have to worry about zombies, but now she needs to get these people to put aside their differences and focus on shared survival.

Another group of refugees reaches the mall, and Ana forces CJ to open the doors so they can rescue them. They get the people inside, but one of the refugees has been bitten, and we all know what that means. The group has to make a difficult decision, one that deeply affects Ana. She won't let a man she's quickly coming to care for kill the infected person, because the infected man has a daughter who will be devastated by his death.

She's still hampered by her training as a nurse, which demands that she preserve life at all costs. But that kind of thinking will get her killed in this new world. It's a weakness, and she knows it. Part of her realizes that he's probably right and she hates herself for thinking that.

We see her begin to set aside her identity as a nurse. She can't always be saving and healing. To survive in this new world she will have to make difficult choices, and this persists through the rest of the Road of Trials.

Shortly thereafter Ana is forced to kill a woman who dies and rises as a zombie. Again and again she is tested. Each time part of her old identity dies, all in preparation for her rebirth into a hero.

The Road of Trials is the first part of the story circle to really deviate from the three-act model. It deviates in the sense that character development is primary. Whatever events occur, they do so with the aim of preparing your character to meet the goddess, and to ultimately rise from the underworld back into the light.

If you recall from the three-act structure, the goal of Act Two was conflict. Contrast the two. Both have conflict, but the Road of Trials has purposeful conflict meant to shape the character in specific ways. Those are the differences, and again why I favor this model.

It isn't just what happens. It's who we become along the way. That isn't perfect for every genre, but if your character needs to grow and change this is an excellent model to follow.

5- Meet the Goddess

Way back during Need, our hero encountered a story problem. They wanted something more than anything in the world, or thought they did. When they meet the (usually metaphorical) goddess, they're granted that desire.

Unfortunately, their Road of Trials has changed them enough to understand that what they thought they wanted isn't what they really want. Instead, they realize that they're after something greater than themselves.

This is a major turning point in the story. After meeting the goddess, the hero will pass from the reactive portion into the proactive. She will begin her ascent back into the light. Doing so will require a conscious, active choice. She is in control now. She is choosing to face her problems, not reacting to them.

> Luke convinces Han and Chewie to help him rescue Leia. He swaggers into her cell feeling like captain badass. He's taken action and done what he originally set out to do, even if he is a little short to be a stormtrooper.
>
> Unfortunately, he still needs to get off the Death Star. Not simply to save Leia, but because R2 contains the plans to the Death Star, and Luke now realizes that the rebels'

only hope is successfully getting the droid back to the alliance.

He gets what he thought he wanted, but in the process learns what he really wants. He has to save the rebels. The mission is more important than him saving the princess. It's even more important than his own life.

Neo meets the Oracle, expecting her to confirm that he's The One. He's not terribly interested in being The One, but until now he's sort of blindly accepted that he must be. The Oracle tells him he isn't. This rocks Neo to the core.

Everything was building to that moment. If he isn't The One, then what is his purpose? The Oracle explains that Morpheus is going to be in a life or death situation, and that if Neo doesn't save him, Morpheus will die. If Neo saves him, he'll sacrifice his own life to do it.

Neo comes to the same realization Luke does. There's something bigger and more important than himself, and he's willing to fight for it.

Ana and the surviving refugees have successfully pushed out the zombies. They have the safety they all craved, what Ana has been seeking since the You step. But she quickly realizes it's an illusion. They can't stay at the mall forever. They'll run out of food, or the zombies will get in.

Safety is, in fact, a prison. One where she will almost certainly die. Ana has safety, but what she really wants is to return to her normal world. She's desperately lost, but still trying to find a way to do that.

It's at this stage the douchey guy (you'll know instantly who he is if you watch the movie) mentions that he owns a boat, and the idea is planted that our heroine could sail off into the sunset, away from the terrible zombies, to safety with a capital S.

She has a new purpose, something she can work actively toward. Something greater than herself, and more important than her own life. This safety isn't just safety for her, it's safety for her friends. Getting there will require her to risk her life, but their collective safety is greater than her own.

Exercise #12- The Second Part of the Circle

Open the story circle document from the last chapter. Under the Road of Trials section, brainstorm three scenes that will bring your character closer to their goal from Need. What trials do they need to face? How are those trials affected by their flaws, and what lessons does this force your character to learn? What external force is propelling them forward?

Define each of these with as much detail as you can muster. It won't all be clear just yet, but hopefully you have some rough ideas.

Now move to the Meet the Goddess step. How can you grant your character what they think they wanted, but also show that they really wanted something else? Consider Star Wars, The Matrix, and Dawn of the Dead and how they did it. Look to your favorite stories. How are they doing it?

Now craft a scene or scenes that will force your character to accept responsibility. They will pass from the passive into the active side of the story circle. They're taking ownership, and actively working to become the person they need to be.

Consider which characters you could add to your plot to fulfill both of these plot points. Who will your protagonist meet? Allies? A mentor? This is your opportunity to add one or more characters.

Bonus: Continue your re-watch / re-read from the last chapter. Watch up to the midpoint of the movie until you've seen / read the Meet the Goddess phase. Did you spot anything that you didn't when analyzing the book for the three-act structure?

13

DAN HARMON'S STORY CIRCLE, PART 3

Okay, we've reached the midpoint of our story. Our character has met their metaphorical (or in the case of my novel, *Void Wyrm*, literal) goddess. They're ready to take responsibility, but what does that entail exactly?

It's time to pay the price for their convictions.

6- Take & Pay

Redemption, at least story redemption, always requires a price. For our hero to reach the light, they must give something up. Often, this means parting with the mentor, or with aid they received during the Road of Trials.

Our hero must learn to stand alone, without the aid he needed in the first half of the story. He's going to beat the enemy on his terms, and is willing to pay the price that requires.

But Take & Pay represents more than that. Through the first half of the book the character has been reactive. They have been static. They have been their old selves, and this has caused a conflict to arise in them.

They now see their new self, the person they have become. But claiming that person will require a price. When the protagonist crosses into Take & Pay, they are symbolically paying the price for their decision.

They have faced their internal conflict, and they have arisen stronger. They have become the hero they need to be. They've passed into the active half of the circle.

> Luke rescues Leia, but just before he reaches the Millennium Falcon, they run into Darth Vader. Obi Wan is getting back at the same time and quickly realizes that the only way Luke can make it off the Death Star is if he sacrifices himself to stall Vader. Luke watches as his mentor is cut down, robbing him of the aid he was given back during the Road of Trials.
>
> He got what he wanted back in Need, but paid a heavy price for it.

> Neo learns that he isn't The One. He gets the information he so desperately wanted. But it turns out he's been betrayed by Cypher. Agents attack, and Morpheus is captured. The price doesn't end there, though. Tank, Dozer, Mouse, and the blonde chick with the sexy accent all die.
>
> Neo got what he wanted, but nearly all of his friends are dead, and now Morpheus has been captured by the enemy. Instead of fleeing from his problems, Neo proves he's become an active hero. He will not back down.

> Ana and her friends launch a daring rescue to get Nicole and her dog back. Several people die in the attempt, but

they save Nicole. Ana got what she wanted, but pays a heavy price to get it.

This is another area where the circle deviates from the three-act structure. In three-act, this would be called the second crisis, and our hero would overcome it by being proactive. That's good, but notice that it doesn't say anything at all about who our hero becomes in the process.

With Take & Pay, your hero has a chance to show that they're human. They deal with loss, but they don't let it stop them from pursuing their ultimate goal. Luke is still trying to fight. Neo is going after Morpheus. Ana is resolved to get her friends safely to the docks, so they can escape the zombies forever.

7- Return

Our heroine has everything she needs. She's paid the price, and is still standing. It's time for the final confrontation with the antagonist. She's been transformed into exactly the person she needs to be to overcome them, and she's about to whoop a whole lot of antagonist-ass.

And she does. For a while. But then there is a reversal. Things suddenly look their darkest.

Luke begins his attack run on the Death Star. He's a confident pilot and he's ready for this. He knows it will probably cost his life, and while he's sad that Han won't be there he understands. This is probably going to be suicide, but there's a chance.

All he has to do is bullseye an impossible shot, just like he used to do all the time back in Beggar's Canyon.

The whole battle following this is all part of return.

The alliance assaults the Death Star, and things are looking grim. Darth Vader has arrived and is picking off X-Wings like he's going for the mythic achievement at his dark lord country club.

Neo launches a daring assault on the Agent stronghold. He and Trinity kick all the ass, and manage to liberate Morpheus. They escape in a helicopter, but the agents shoot it down. It's crashing, but somehow Neo saves everyone anyway. Because he's the frigging One and we all know it. He even moves like the agents now.

But then they're jumped by Agent Smith. Trinity gets out, but Smith shoots the phone and Neo is trapped inside the Matrix. There's no escape. Neo brawls with Smith, and to our surprise and delight, he just barely wins.

But then Agent Smith comes back in another body, and now he has two friends with him. Neo is outnumbered and outgunned. Things have never looked so bleak.

Ana and her friends take a pair of armored busses out into the sea of zombies. They cut a path through them, racing toward the docks as quickly as they can. They're going to make it!

Oops, no they aren't. One of the busses crashes, and it's the one with the key to the boat they're going to use to escape.

Ana has to stop her bus, and get out to rescue her friends. She's surrounded by a sea of zombies. They're closing in on all sides.

Notice that in every case our hero is in mortal peril. They're facing their darkest fear, and they've been stripped of their outside help. They've reached the darkest moment. In a romance, this might be the moment where the protagonist is pleading his case to the love interest, who is furious with him.

8- Changed

Fortunately, our hero is no longer the same person they were in You. They've spent the entire book changing and growing, and are now able to deal with the problems that their old selves would not have been able to solve.

This is their chance to prove that they've changed, to show that their transformation is complete. By the end, they will have completed their quest and be ready to return to whatever version of their ordinary world still exists.

They confront the story problem, usually an external force in the form of the antagonist, and they overcome that force. Whereas crossing into Take & Pay represented overcoming internal conflict, Changed is all about overcoming the external.

Luke shows that he's no longer the naive young farm boy, and that he's learned to trust the force. He turns off his targeting computer, removing his 'supernatural aid', and uses the force to make the shot.

The Death Star blows up. The alliance survives. Luke has become the hero he needed to be, and has saved everyone.

Neo dies. But ultimately, The One has power over life and death. So Neo resurrects and casually destroys Agent Smith. We see that he has changed, so much so that when he views the matrix he now sees code instead of the world as we see it.

Neo has effectively become a god in the matrix, and can now begin the work of freeing the human race from the machines.

Earlier we talked a little about the story question, and in this case the question is 'what is the Matrix?' We were **told** what it was when Neo took the red pill, but only when Neo actually sees the code does he finally **know** what the Matrix is.

Ana and her companions reach the dock. They fight off the last wave of zombies, and make it onto the boat. Because this is a horror movie, the ending is bittersweet. Ana loses Michael, and in the process shows that she has changed.

The woman she's become is strong enough to survive in this new world, and we're left with a sense of hope for her future.

In each case, the hero or heroine accomplishes their quest. They vanquish their opponent. They get the guy. They get the job. They save the world. They find safety. Whatever the needs of your genre, they just knocked it out of the park.

In the process, they became something greater and we got to ride shotgun. This is why endings can have such an amazing payoff. Reach back to your childhood and see if you can remember the sense of elation when the Death Star exploded.

I cheered out loud. I still do sometimes. Because I'm invested in Luke. Because I've grown up alongside him during the story. I've seen him descend into the underworld to grow, and change, and then return into the light.

Exercise #13- The Third Part of the Circle

Get out your story circle document, and add your Take & Pay. What is all this going to cost your heroine? What does she lose? Does this require you to add a setup earlier in the book? Modify the earlier sections of the document if needed.

If you remember from the LAYER step, we added a Return. Compare the original with your ending in the three-act document. After reading both, write your Return step using what you've read in this chapter. What is the final confrontation? And how can you make things look their bleakest, just before the inevitable victory in Changed?

Now add your Changed step, and bring it all together. This is the ultimate payoff that you first envisioned back in the LAYER step. Are you offering a satisfying conclusion? Are you paying off all the setups? Most importantly, has your character transformed into the heroine they need to be?

Bonus: Finish your re-watch / re-read. Open a fresh document, and write out your thoughts about the story. Did it follow the story circle? Were you able to spot all the plot points? Pick a book or movie you think is bad, and perform exactly the same kind of analysis. Where do they mess up and why?

14

LAYING OUT SCENES

W e're nearing the end of Part 4. You've learned two different story structures, and I'm hoping one of them interests you enough to try. If you're writing in a genre where your protagonist doesn't need to transform, then I'd recommend the three-act structure.

Otherwise, I'd pick the story circle. Either way, we're going to need to lay out scenes. Some of the exercises have already had you create placeholder documents, but this is our chance to expand that list into enough scenes to support an entire novel.

Here's how we do that.

Laying Out the Scenes

In the previous few chapters, we finished your first story circle. I'll often do one for each point of view character, and recommend you do the same.

Once I have my story circle(s) created, I take the information from each plot point and break them down into scenes. Each scene gets its own document file in Scrivener.

I create a folder for each plot point, then drop one or more scenes into the folder that correspond to what I've written. Is that plot point just one scene, or will it require three scenes to really do it justice? If so, I create three documents.

You'll notice in the screenshot below that each scene has the name of its corresponding PoV character. I group them this way, because when I do the actual writing I tend to stick with one PoV and write as many of their chapters as I can before switching to another PoV.

If this seems counterintuitive, you can name the documents however you'd like.

These scene documents are simple, usually containing one paragraph, or even a single sentence description of the scene.

Aran fights the binder and his armor is damaged.

Voria stands trial and is stripped of both her dignity and rank. Her father will intervene.

Once I've laid out all the scenes for the first story circle,

I'll repeat this process until I have scenes from all PoV characters, including the antagonist. Then I'll go back to the first scene and start reading. I'll spend a few minutes with each scene document, going over the techniques below to flesh out each document into a full scene.

Types of Scenes

A few years back I heard a podcast with Russell Blake where he laid out the types of scenes he used. It was one of those eye-opening moments, and as soon as I understood what he meant, my scenes improved dramatically. This was what was missing when I'd written my first novel.

I've always been told that you have action scenes and reaction scenes. That makes sense, but it only gives a general sense of what's involved in a scene. I figured it meant if there was a fight, or some sort of high conflict, it was action. Otherwise it was reaction. I tried to have more action than reaction, figuring that made for a more exciting novel.

That put me ahead of where I was, but it still limited my scenes to just two types. That gave me less control than I was after, but thankfully, Russell's interview taught me that scenes can be broken into four types:

- A = Action
- S = Surprise / Revelation
- N = Need / Question
- R = Reversal / Big Reveal

This is an extremely useful way of looking at scene structure, and makes it easy to see at a glance how a list of scenes serve the needs of the story. Action scenes are exactly what they sound like. Surprise / Revelation gives a plot reveal. Need / Question has our protagonist trying to obtain something, either a physical object or simply information.

A reversal or big reveal usually happens right around the Return plot point, and I only have 1-2 per book. These are your big aha, or whoah moments that the rest of the plot turns on. Han returning to save Luke. Neo rising from the dead. Ana finding out that Michael has been bitten.

I lay out my scenes using the story circles, and then I go through and identify each. If you're writing fast paced science fiction like I am, then you need to make sure you have a certain amount of A scenes. If you're writing a cozy mystery you need to rely on more S, N, and R scenes.

I look through my plots, and start making modifications based on the genre. Oh, I need a chase scene here (A). We need a reveal about Voria's parents here (S), and later we need to find out that Aran's entire life has been manipulated (R).

This leaves me with 50-60 scene placeholders created from my various story circles, plus a few more from adding scenes I think are either cool or necessary.

Fleshing Out Scene Descriptions

Once I've got all my scene placeholders I begin with the first scene, and start fleshing them out, one after another. Where is this scene set? Who are the characters involved? What time of day is it? Where is everyone emotionally? Much of this is mental and not written down, but I do jot down the most important parts:

- Time and Environment: *Takes place aboard the Big Texas, in the mess. Dusk. Chilly. Parked at starport.*

- Characters involved: *Aran, Voria, Ikadra, random waitress.*
- Scene need: (R) *Crewes reveals he's still alive and attacks Dirk from behind.*

Basically, I need enough information to know where the scene is happening, and that means having a few details to impart to the reader. I need to know who is involved in the scene, and what each person wants. That will tell me where the conflict lies, which will help me craft appropriate dialogue from the characters involved.

I repeat this for every scene in the book before sitting down to write any of them, but usually by the time I do this I've done several versions of the story circle document. I make sure I know where the story is going before making the individual scenes.

I will often find that a scene no longer makes sense, or needs to be expanded or changed, or just moved around in the order. Keeping simple placeholders makes this easy to do, and I treat my outline as a living thing, even after I start writing the book.

The goal for this stage is just to get a complete story in place, even if that complete story has big, glaring plot holes.

Exercise #14- Outline Your Novel

This is the big one. We've gradually given you all the basic tools necessary to outline your novel. Take every document you've created and arrange them into either the three-act structure or the story circle as shown in my screenshot above. It's totally okay (and expected) for there to be gaps at this point.

Go through every single document and lay out the scene using the technique in this chapter. Where does it take place? Who is the PoV character? What type of scene is it? Add the corresponding letter to your scene.

I highly recommend doing the bonus step as well. This exercise might only be a couple hundred words long, but what I'm asking you to do can be a monumental undertaking. It may mean weeks of adding documents and changing descriptions.

That's totally okay. Your outline is a living, breathing thing that will change over time. All you're doing here is completing the first draft.

Bonus: Consider the needs of your genre. Do you have enough A scenes? Do you have 1-2 Rs? Do you need more Ss? Tweak your outline to include these additional scenes.

Once you're finished, read the outline from the top. How does it sound?

PART V

TENDING YOUR GARDEN

15

PLOT BRANCHING

Congratulations! You've created your first outline, assuming you've done the exercises. Now it's time to dive back into the creative side of things. Before we do so, though, you need to ask yourself The Big Question (tm).

Are you ready to write this novel?

For some people the answer will be yes, even though the outline is still incomplete. There's enough there that they can start writing, and the act of discovery writing will teach those writers more about the plot.

If that's you, then knock yourself out. Write a few chapters and see how it feels.

If you don't feel at all prepared to start writing, that's totally okay too. Either way we still have a ton of work left to do.

Gardeners don't just plant seeds, and then show up a couple months later to harvest their corn. They tend those plants every day. They look for pests. They water them.

We need to do the same thing to our novel. We need to

spend time every day asking ourselves questions. We always want to deepen our understanding of the characters, their motivation, and the world they live in.

To do this, I'll set the outline aside for a week. When I come back I go through every scene and ask the following questions:

- Does everyone's motivation make sense?
- Does the conflict make sense? Why is the protagonist invested? What's at stake if they lose?
- What are the coolest scenes? Why are those scenes cooler than the rest? Can I add something to the other scenes to bring them up to the same level? Can I change the location? Can I add an emergency, or raise the stakes in some way?
- Does every scene have the right level of conflict, or are my characters buddy buddy all the time? What is their stress level like? Can I raise conflict and / or tension?
- Conversely, do I have enough of the other scene types? It can't be all action.
- Are my characters sympathetic? Active? Do they grow?
- How can I make the situation worse?

Each time I perform this exercise I add definition to existing scenes. I'll also brainstorm new characters, new scenes, and new parts of the world.

Any changes I make to various chapter outlines can invalidate later sections of the book, and that's okay. It's much better to do this now, rather than writing the scenes and deciding I don't need those 20,000 words because the plot is different now.

We're in the planning phase, and now is the time to make changes. If you think a character wouldn't behave a certain way, even though the plot says they need to, then perhaps the plot needs to change.

Your entire goal, as stated earlier, is to learn about the characters. Readers stay for characters. Great books arise from character. Don't let them be slaves to plot. Make them part of it.

Plot Branching

One of the final exercises I do is to ask, 'what's the worst thing that could happen in this scene?' When asking this question, it's vital you know what would most scare the PoV character, what would raise the stakes the most.

Most new authors, myself included, tend to go with our first idea. Resist that impulse. Instead, create several options for key scenes, then consider how each would impact the plot. Some of the resulting plots won't make any sense, or won't work. But some might be better than your initial ideas.

If it's unclear how this process is used, let's apply it to Star Wars. We ask a question that would change the story in some fundamental way.

What if Leia died instead of Obi Wan?

That's a simple, powerful question. If Leia had died getting off the Death Star and Obi Wan had lived, then Luke wouldn't have lost his mentor. Obi Wan would have been around to guide the alliance. He'd have been able to help plan the attack with the Death Star.

But this would also have had tremendous repercussions internally for our hero. How would Luke have reacted? We saw his moment of grief when his mentor died. Would it have been better or worse if it had been Leia? What if Ben revealed that she was really his sister?

I often end up with six or seven versions of my story circle documents, and each is created through a plot branching exercise. In my *Void Wraith* trilogy, one of my protagonists sacrifices himself by slamming his ship into the enemy. Poor Khar was doomed.

Then I did a plot branching exercise, and I wrote out a version of the plot where he never sacrificed himself. The bad guys won, so that wasn't going to work. I scrapped it and wrote another. This time I had Khar live. He sacrificed his ship, but Khar is a cyborg and can survive in a vacuum.

In the end I went with that last version. Had I not performed the exercise, Khar would have died. Instead, he went on to become the star of the next series.

Plot branches may or may not get used. Some will be ludicrous. Some might break the story. But some will be better than your initial ideas, and will result in a stronger plot. I encourage you to always ask how a scene can be different, and how making it different will affect your larger plot.

~

Exercise #15- Add a Plot Branch

Add three plot branches to your Take & Pay step. What if the story veered off in another direction? Consider ways it could go very badly, or humorously, or favorably. Which fits the tone of the book you're after? Which best informs the character you're creating?

Modify the outline to include the changes.

Bonus: Repeat this process with your Return step. Create a reminder for one week. Re-read all versions you've created, then re-write one final version.

16

CULTIVATING CHARACTERS

Back in Chapter 5 and Chapter 6, we talked about characters. We went over the four pillars and layering in flaws. Over the course of the book, there were several points where you were asked to consider adding a mentor or an ally.

Before you begin writing in earnest, it's important to understand these characters, and any others that you write. Fleshing out the outline has started that process, and hopefully you've got some notes, but it's important to realize that how well you write the characters determines a large part of how strong the ultimate story is.

We've all seen movies or read stories that had such an amazing premise, but the execution was lacking. At the time we might not have been able to pinpoint the reason, but in many cases it's the characters. If the characters are weak, uninteresting, or unsympathetic, then we won't fully engage with the story.

The awesome setting, be it Hawaii, inside the matrix, or on Tatooine, is ultimately meaningless unless we care about the people we're riding shotgun with. The more you know about your characters, the easier it will be to get the reader to care about them.

We tend to accept people we understand, and fear people we do not. It's human nature, a leftover survival instinct from our time on the plains of Africa over a hundred millennia ago. This is why we eventually come to care for monsters like Jaime Lannister.

The very first scene in *A Game of Thrones* shows him having sex with his sister, and when he's discovered, Jaime shoves an eight-year-old child out a tower window to the unforgiving stone below. This dude is messed up. Yet by the 5th book I am genuinely horrified to realize that I'm rooting for Jaime.

Because after hundreds of pages of seeing him make difficult decisions, and hearing about the terrible experiences that shaped his childhood, I know him. I understand him. He's despicable, but he's part of my tribe, and I want him to become a better person.

Jaime is a great character, because he's interesting and complex. He isn't perfect. He isn't even good. But he's right for the story he's in. You want to aim for the same thing, characters that fit the story.

I will do a full book on characters one day, but for now here are the last few tips I can offer for building your characters before you start the actual writing.

Context

So how do you get people to care about characters? The first way is through context. If our protagonist is a beer-swilling mercenary with a mean streak, and we put in him in a scene with a likable corporal doing the right thing, then the reader is probably going to dislike our merc.

If we show him next to several mercs that are even worse, and it becomes clear that our beer swilling mercenary is a shade more likable than they are, we'll start to identify with him immediately. He's the best option in that situation, because we've crafted the scene to allow the reader no better choice.

Going back to our *Game of Thrones* example, I really disliked Jaime when I met him, for good reason. He's a despicable bastard, especially since we're contrasting him to Ned Stark, a pure and noble lord. However, he doesn't hold a candle to his own son, Joffrey. Joffrey is a true monster, and when he becomes king, he abuses that power in ways that make even Jaime pause. Joffrey's very existence softens Jaime's. Martin didn't have to do anything at all other than show Jaime's horror at his own son. We realize that there's something far, far worse, and so Jaime can't be that bad, right?

Humans are interesting that way.

When you're constructing your antagonists consider their context with the protagonist, and with other antagonists. If the protagonist's mentor is frightened by the big bad, then our protagonist will know he should be terrified, through context.

Every character in your novel will reflect on the other characters, so consider carefully how their relationships and perceptions of each other might read. Your readers certainly will, whether they realize it or not.

Characters That Won't Behave

One of the biggest problems I run into is characters that won't behave. I create them for a specific plot purpose, but through chance they sometimes come to life on their own. If you're a meticulous plotter, you quash these characters and force them right back into their molds.

Sometimes that makes sense, but in most cases I let creativity reign. I'll consider this new direction for the character, who may surprise me even while I'm writing them. Rather than abandoning my wayward character, or forcing them back to the mold, I instead spend a while considering the ramifications of the change.

This has happened to me twice in recent projects. In plotting *The Dark Lord Bert*, I'd originally intended my protagonist to be a human moisture farmer as a sort of play on Star Wars. During the course of creating support characters, I made Bert, a goblin who lived at the local dump.

The problem was that Bert was a whole lot more sympathetic than my intended protagonist. He was funnier, naturally flawed, and had the best available character arc. Bert quickly stole the entire plot, and within a few days he was my new protagonist. I didn't try to stop Bert. I followed to see where he'd lead. I'm so glad I did.

You have to make the call on when to rein in a character. If they're wrecking your plot, then do what you have to, even if it means changing that character. But at least consider whether this new direction you've selected might be a better route and make for a richer character. Your readers will thank you for it.

Condensing Characters

One of the mistakes I've made in several series is character bloat. Every book adds a few new characters, and the cast gets to the point where even the author has trouble keeping track of everything.

That's expected in a series, to an extent, but we can minimize it by condensing characters. Do you have two small roles at different points in the novel, both played by forgettable characters that are little more than a name?

What if both characters were replaced by Beth, who happens to be your protagonist's cousin, so she's got that relationship too. Instead of a throwaway character, you can create a likable secondary character by condensing several small roles. This character can recur through the series whenever you need a specific kind of secondary character.

This reduces the number of characters the reader keeps track of, and the deeper you get into a series the more they will thank you for this. I'm looking at you, Wheel of Time, with your 147 PoV characters. That isn't an exaggeration. It really has 147 characters, and it could easily have been condensed to half that number without sacrificing much plot.

Keep it simple, and make every character significant. This will give people one more hook to latch onto, and the more you do that, the more time they want to spend in your world.

Symbolic Representation

My final tip for cultivating characters is another brain-science-y one. Humans are masters of symbolic representation. If you see a red octagon in the United States your brain tells you STOP. We link meaning and emotion to symbols, and most of us are very visual.

All this writing stuff exists, at first, only in our heads. Making it real outside our heads can strengthen our writing immeasurably. You know all those crime dramas where the hero has this board on the wall with lines connecting all the important events? That works for a reason. It extends the problem beyond our own heads, and lets us view it from different angles.

So what does that have to do with characters? Each character is a series of labels, or symbols, stored in your reader's head. All you need to do is provide the right symbols, and the reader will do the rest.

Of course, to do that you first need to have created those symbols in your own brain. You have to think like a reader. I begin this process by Googling artwork to represent every one of my characters, because me understanding what characters look like is necessary to convey that to the reader. I'm a visual person.

If you're writing a sports romance, then look up hot soccer player. Find the one who most embodies your love interest, and download that image. If you're using Word or Scrivener you can drop it right into the character document.

You will be amazed how quickly that character comes to life, simply because you've provided your brain an anchor. The very first label you've associated with that character is 'hot soccer player picture', and when you think of that character, that's the visual your brain will provide.

Plus, it's really fun to go searching for images to represent cool stuff and people in your world. Note that I'm not suggesting you use this artwork for any purpose other than your own edification. If you post it anywhere, or use it publicly in any way, make sure you get permission and credit the artist.

But dropping it into Scrivener is just fine, and immensely helpful to the creative process.

∾

Exercise #16- Cultivate Some Characters

Go through your entire outline and generate a working list of characters for your novel in your format of choice. I use the Character section of Scrivener for this, but if Index cards work for you, that's fine. Anything that generates a complete list is acceptable.

Make a list of labels or symbols associated with each character. Are they tall? Are they a know-it-all? Consider each character. Then, and only then, go out and find artwork for each and drop it into the file, or print it out if you're doing analogue.

Set a reminder for tomorrow at an appropriate time. Review each character, and take a moment to stare at each image you downloaded. Say the character's name out loud as you're staring at the image.

This process will force your brain to create a sort of person symbol for each character, making them just as real as the people you actually know.

Bonus: Write a paragraph in each character file from the perspective of the character. What does their dialogue sound like? What concerns do they have on a daily basis? How are they different from you?

17

PLANNING THE NEXT HARVEST

This is the last meaty chapter in the book. I put it at the end, because it's the last big concern you need to address before sitting down to write your novel. Is there going to be a sequel, or many sequels? Or are you writing a standalone novel?

If you're writing a long running series, then there are a few additional concerns beyond simply plotting the novel. You need to plant seeds for future books, which you can only do if you have some idea what those future books might contain.

If your novel is the first in a series, then what kind of series is it? Are we talking a bunch of standalone books where the protagonist doesn't change much, like Ms. Marple or Sherlock Holmes? Or does the hero have a slow burn arc like they do in Jim Butcher's *Dresden Files*?

If you have very little character development from book to book, then you're in the clear. You can happily crank out stand alone novels using the same character with only minor variations from book to book. This is especially common in Action and Adventure with characters like Jack

Ryan, or Tom Cruise in *Mission Impossible*, since he's basically playing himself.

These characters don't grow or change much installment to installment, but we know going in that we're going to see them solve a case, or save the world, or make us laugh if it's a comedy series. And many readers are just fine with that. Not every story has to be a hero's journey.

But what if your series is? What if you're following a billion book cycle? How do you keep your character growing?

Little Changes

Dan Harmon's first big success was a half hour episodic comedy called Community. It's about a bunch of very flawed people muddling their way through a local community college, and every single 22-minute episode was written using the story circle.

The idea is that a character needs to learn or change in a small way each episode. Not every character every episode, but one character every episode. By the end of the series, Jeff Winger, arguably the protagonist, has gone from a completely selfish ass to a caring friend and supportive mentor.

This doesn't happen in any single episode. Each episode has him learning a tiny lesson, or seeing a situation in a new way. Over a long series, we can endeavor to do the same.

In my military SF series, the main protagonist always kicks a whole lot of butt. Fans know this going in, and know that Nolan's going to be put in situations that will test him to the limits. He will need to come up with an inventive solution to overcome a vastly superior foe.

Readers expect that in every book, and if that's all I gave

them they'd probably come back for more. But it isn't. Over six books, Nolan has learned to stop thinking so much about tactics, and to start thinking like a strategist. He becomes more of a leader, and learns to think longer term.

Every time I write another book in his series, I make sure to have a story circle written. Nolan is going to change and grow in some way, though that may be a small amount of growth.

Now granted, I haven't written a 25-book series. The longest I've done is six books, but in that series I'm only scratching the surface of development for this character.

The trick is deciding on one small realistic change each book. Instead of something broad like 'Nolan will become an amazing strategist', I'll do something more basic. In *Destroyer*, Nolan learns that he can't trust the command structure and needs to think for himself. In *Void Wraith*, Nolan learns that sometimes you need to expose yourself to risk by trusting a former enemy. In *Eradication*, Nolan learns that he can't do everything himself. Sometimes you need to delegate.

See the pattern? Nolan is learning like a real person. Think back to school, ideally college or university if you attended. If not, high school or your equivalent is fine. Think about your freshman year and who you were. Then think about yourself in your senior year.

During those fours years you learned tons of lessons. It wasn't a single turning point, but rather a series of revelations. That's how we all grow up, and we can do the same thing over a long series.

Use small lessons.

Begin With the End

I keep going back to Jim Butcher's *Dresden Files* because it's the longest running series that has me willing to pay any cover price on release day. I'll shell out $17.99 for an ebook, and do it happily just so I can immerse myself in the next book.

Jim has done many interviews about the series, and has been very clear for years. He might not know exactly what the next several books hold, but he absolutely knows the ending of his 20+ book series. He's known it since the first book.

The Dresden Files is being set up to have an epic war between titanic forces, and it's been done piece by piece, book by book, for over a decade. None of the books deal specifically with this war. Each has their own plot needs, and a case that is solved by the end of the book.

But they are all also clearly moving in a pre-planned direction, one that will maneuver all the players into the right positions in time for our epic ending.

I used this process both with my *Deathless* series, and my *Magitech Chronicles*. The *Magitech Chronicles* are broken into two arcs, The Krox (books 1-5), and Nefarius (6-10). I've planned a third arc, but odds are good by that point it will make sense to launch it as a separate series.

I know where everyone has to be by the end of each arc, and I know where they start out. All I have to do is connect the dots.

For *Deathless*, I had one six-book arc, but I've known since the first book precisely how I would end the series. I have always worked toward that point. *Deathless* was plotted used the three-act structure, and the *Magitech Chronicles* are plotted using Dan Harmon's Story Circle.

I also have the *Void Wraith* trilogy, and when I wrote that, I did it with much less idea where the series would end. I only had a vague premise, and without the clear target, the series suffered. It's sold really well and people enjoyed it, but I know it could have been more if I'd had a better idea of where I was going when I started.

I made mistakes in that series. Mistakes that could have been avoided if I knew the ending before I started writing.

Expand Your Cast

One of the reasons fans so love *A Song of Ice and Fire* and the corresponding HBO show *Game of Thrones* is that there is a rich cast of characters. Off the top of my head, I love Tyrion, Danerys, Arya, and surprisingly Jaime.

Other people I talk to all have their own favorite characters. Some like Jon, or the Hound, or Tywin. Some even like Cersei. We each connect for different reasons, but almost everyone finds a character they can identify with.

We can do the same thing in our own series. Having many PoV characters makes it more likely that a reader will connect with one. More importantly, it allows you to have more than one character undergo a character arc.

If you've got six point of view characters, you're going to get a lot more mileage out of their development than someone writing from a single point of view. However, this expansion is a useful tool even if you have the same PoV for every book, like the Dresden Files.

You can expand the cast of characters that your protagonists meet. The more alliances, rivalries, and enemies that a character has, the easier your series is to sustain. What's more, any character can be changed at any time. Yesterday's enemy is tomorrow's ally, and vice versa.

This constantly shifting landscape across a variety of characters will sustain reader interest indefinitely, as long as those characters are slowly growing and changing.

Exercise #17- The Last One

If you are planning on writing a series, then choose a type. Are you writing an epic, or a series of standalone novels? If it's standalones, have a high five and skip this exercise. If it's an epic, then put on your gloves because we're about to do some gardening.

Spend a moment considering the epic ending of your series. What might it look like? This is just a thought experiment, and is likely to change several times. For now, just pick something that sounds cool, and run with it. Will your character conquer the world? Become president? Get her own talk show and become bigger than Oprah?

Once you have an idea, think about the timeframe. How far away is this hypothetical future? A year? Five? Sixty? Pick something appropriate to your genre and setting. How might your character change between now and then? Who will they have to become, and what will they have to master to be this dream version of themselves? Start jotting down notes on their character sheet.

Now take a look at your cast as a whole. How will the existing cast develop over the series? Repeat the process with each of them until you have a rough idea of how each will grow and change throughout the series.

Bonus: Pick a long-running series in the same genre as your novel, ideally one you haven't read. Start reading it. As you do so, take special note of each protagonist in the novel, and when you finish each book take the time to write down how you think each grew or changed. Did you find that growth satisfying? Which characters do you like?

Repeat this until you've done a case study on every book in the series. How did the author handle their character arcs? Did the series sustain your interest? Why or why not?

18

THE LAST CHAPTER

A s those of you who've followed the *Write Faster, Write Smarter* series know, this is always my favorite chapter to write. This is my open dialogue with authors, and represents a chance to talk about the industry, and our place in it. It's reserved for people who've reached the end of one of my books, and have hopefully learned something in the process.

This time, I want to talk about the future. Your future, specifically. I'm now well known enough that I get tagged a lot on Facebook, in a variety of author groups. I've withdrawn from social media, for the most part, but I do still read and comment occasionally.

I see the concerns in these groups, and the questions I hear most often always center around the same thing. People fear the future. They worry that the market is getting too crowded, or that their next book won't do well.

It's impossible not to worry about those things, since both influence whether or not we'll be able to do this author thing for a living. At the same time, you have control over your focus. You have control over your mindset. You are the master of your own thoughts.

There's so much pressure in the indie world to get books out faster. But me? I'm slowing down. Don't get me wrong, I'm still writing my 7,000 words a day. But I'm taking my time publishing, and putting out fewer books.

I'm able to do that, because I have fifteen novels out. Because I've paid my dues, and learned the ropes. Because my writing is getting better.

If I could go back to Chris from three years ago, I would have advised patience. You don't have to conquer the world tomorrow, and many success stories are people quietly toiling in the trenches for years before their big break. *Wool* was something like Hugh Howey's eighth novel. *The Martian* was out for years before it took off.

You can't really control the future. But you can control the present. You can work your tail off to become a better writer. You can master story structure, and get in the habit of writing fast, every day. If you do those things, well that's the recipe for a career novelist.

But getting there will take time, and persistence. It will mean not giving up when it gets hard, or when you make an embarrassing mistake (and we all do). It will mean admitting your weaknesses, and working diligently to correct them.

I'm still learning about story and about character. I still read every book that comes out on either subject in the desperate quest for that nugget of new understanding. I recommend you do the same. I hope this book serves as a launch pad, and gets you thinking about story.

At the end of the day, though, this is just a book, and not a terribly long one. It can help your understanding of story, but the only thing that will truly matter is practice. You must write your own stories, if you wish to master craft. And you must study other stories.

To that end, please do the exercises. They're compiled in the next chapter, and while they will take you a while, at the end of the process you will have a full outline and be ready to dive into your novel at *5,000 Words Per Hour* (see what I did there?).

If you run into obstacles, then look for the resources to overcome them. That could be a book, or a video, or a conversation with an author you respect. There are six more books in this series that address most of the specific needs authors face, from producing more words, to figuring out how to sell your books.

Take the path that works for you.

Since many people ask, yes I do story consulting, as well as launch consulting. I charge a lot. There are far less expensive resources, and I don't think I'm worth your money until you've spent time exhausting them.

But, if you're convinced you're at a stage where you think you want help fine tuning your work reach out to me at chris@chrisfoxwrites.com. I'm always happy to help.

In the meantime, I'm going to get back to the writing. It still blows me away how far I've come since I first published *5,000 Words Per Hour* in 2015. I always wanted to be an author, but I never expected I'd become a teacher.

Thanking for sticking with me, and for listening to what I have to say. Now get out there and write the best novel you can. =D

-Chris

EXERCISES

Exercise #1- Set Up a Planter Box

Before we can start gardening, we need a place to garden. You need to pick a way to organize your novel, be it Scrivener (which I use), Evernote, Word, Ulysses, or anything else that works for you. Whatever you pick, know that organization is key. You want separate boxes for the following:

- Scenes / Chapters
- Characters
- Locations
- Research

Some authors prefer more, and some less. Experiment until you find which works for you. I'm still adjusting my process and the more I do it, the more efficient I've become.

Bonus: Go watch the first *How To Plot Your Novel From*

Scratch video located at youtube.com/chrisfoxwrites. There are a total of five videos, and they're about 7 minutes each.

Exercise #2- Add Some Soil

Create a document in your Planter Box and use the LAYER technique to generate the first layer of soil. This first version should only be a few paragraphs long, as my example was. If you're inspired to make it longer, though, don't censor yourself.

Bonus: Spend some extra time fleshing out your Yard. What is your world like? Are there powers or abilities? If this is a detective story, what sets it apart from other detective stories? Brainstorm three unique concepts, places, inventions, or characters and add those documents to your planter box.

Exercise #3- Setup Your Payoffs

Take a look at your Return from the last chapter. What elements need to be properly setup? Create a chapter placeholder document for the ultimate payoff, and then one for each setup you brainstorm.

Pick a point of view for each of these scenes. Who might have the most to lose, and why? Do you need scenes from your antagonist's PoV? Create appropriate chapter placeholders in your planter box.

Bonus: Brainstorm three reaction scenes to sprinkle around the chapters you've already created. If your character experiences a setback, how does that impact them? They just got rejected by their love interest, or they discovered a clue to the murder. How do they react? What do they decide to do to further pursue their goal?

Exercise #4- Make Them Feel

Go through each of the scene placeholders you've created, and pick an emotional resonance. Is the scene going to make the reader feel frustrated? Sad? Angry? Amused? Remember when we said that each beat is defined by its emotional resonance?

It's time to add those definitions to the scenes you've created. When you're done you should have something like this. These are chapter names from *The Dark Lord Bert.*

- Typical Adventurers (Action, Amusement)
- Paradise (Reaction, Curious)
- The Attack (Action, Outrage)
- Boberton (Reaction, Resolve)

Bonus: It's time to use your Pacing tool. Lay your scenes out chronologically, and review the emotions you've added. If you want to build up to an incredible climax, you're going to need a number of scenes to ramp up the tension. Define three new scenes and fit them into the plot to help you do this.

If it's unclear which scenes you should add, ask yourself

how you can make the situation worse. Always make it worse, so that in the end you can make it better. Setups and payoffs.

~

Exercise #5- Flesh Out Your Protagonist

Take a look at the paragraph you wrote about your protagonist. Are they sympathetic? Will readers understand why they are doing what they are doing? This requires you to understand your character's motivation. So define that now. Think about the rough ending of your book. Why does your character want to get there? And what's on the line if they fail?

Now brainstorm three scenes, or add to existing scenes, where your hero is moving closer to their goal. These core scenes should show the reader who your character is, and what they are made of. It should show them active.

Finally, ask yourself about your protagonist. How is she different at the end? What's changed? Did she grow? Add any setups to earlier chapters, or make new chapters for those setups.

Bonus: Add a save the cat scene early in the book. What can your character do to demonstrate their competence and compassion (assuming they have one or both).

~

Exercise #6- Layer in Character Flaws

Make a list of three potential flaws in each category for your character. Consider which of these flaws would impact them the most in their setting. Being a slave won't mean much if they live in a colony of slaves. It most definitely would in pre-civil war America.

Choose one flaw from each category, and layer them into the character. Consider what made your character the way they are. Why do they have these flaws?

Most importantly, consider how these flaws can be lessened or removed by the end of the book. Not every character has to deal with flaws, and in fact doing so can be disingenuous. Wolverine will always be a grumpy anti-hero. But if the flaws can be faced and then overcome, how are you planning to do it?

Add appropriate setups and payoffs to your planter box for each flaw.

Bonus: Repeat this process for the antagonist. In many ways they should be a stronger mirror of your protagonist. If we're writing a romantic comedy for example, which flaws you choose can really help you amp up the humor.

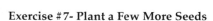

Exercise #7- Plant a Few More Seeds

Consider each of the flaws you added to the protagonist in the last chapter. Envision a way to express each to the reader without ever coming right out saying what it is. Your goal is to get the reader to append the right label all on their own.

If your character has the psychological flaw TIMID, then

how does that manifest? Does he avoid eye contact? Does he have the right answer to a question in class, but is too frightened to speak up when the teacher asks, thereby allowing the antagonist to answer it for him?

Repeat this for each flaw, in each category. Now take a look at your chapter placeholders. When in the story does each of these flaws need to be set up? Create placeholders for each of the chapters you've brainstormed, or add notes to existing scenes if it makes sense to reveal those flaws there.

Remember that the goal is to get the character to say, "oh, that's the clumsy girl." You never want to tell them she's clumsy. Show them by having her spill her drink, and they'll generate their own label.

Bonus: Create an ally / friend / sidekick for your protagonist. Repeat exercises #5 and #6 to define them, then repeat this exercise to decide how you will reveal their flaws and personality to the reader.

≈

Exercise #8- Adding More Soil

What makes your world unique? Do you have magic? Super technology? Or is it a cozy mystery set in an exotic location on another continent?

Generate a list of things you'll need to flesh out to bring that world to life.

If you're writing that cozy mystery, ask yourself the questions a traveler would ask. Does your exotic location have internet access? How do the locals travel? By boat? Foot? How do these things influence the local culture? What sort of character(s) might live there? What would the locals' daily concerns be? How do people earn their living?

If you're writing SF&F and have magic, or some sort of technology that doesn't exist in our world, how does that change things? What are the ramifications of this technology? How would people use it for profit? What would change if everyone had access to it? Warfare? The economy? Space travel?

Generate a list of things that will be different about the setting, and write a paragraph describing each.

Bonus: If you are an SF&F author, pick an exotic real world location and flesh out all the ordinary things about it, as described above. If you are any other type of author, create a radical magic or technology and add it to your world, even if you don't plan on using it in the novel. Consider how that might affect your characters' lives, the global economy, or how various religions might react.

What are the ramifications? Answering these questions will tell you a great deal about your world.

Exercise #9- Fertilize that Soil

One of the best ways to get your subconscious churning is by studying work you love. Pick the book or movie you are most familiar with in the list above and buy or borrow a copy. The idea is to take something you've already seen, and to watch or read it again with a critical eye, now understanding how story structure works.

For this exercise all you need to do is acquire the book or movie. You can watch it if you'd like, but if you do so before reading the next couple chapters, then I'd encourage you to watch it again afterwards.

Bonus: Pick something from the list you aren't familiar with and buy or borrow it.

~

Exercise # 10- Add the Three-Act Structure

Create a new document in your planter box and label it Three-Act Structure. Write a short description of each plot point. They don't have to be much longer than what we created back in the LAYER step.

You don't need to make chapter placeholders yet, because you may not end up using this structure. In the next chapter we'll be creating a mirror using the story circle. Only then will you decide which you prefer.

For now, just create this single document. Give each plot point as much time and attention as it needs, and as you're doing so, always be asking questions. Do you need to add characters to the plot to make each point work? Which ones come naturally, and which have you scratching your head?

You may not be able to finish this exercise quickly, and on the first pass it's totally acceptable to put a ??? under a plot point you aren't sure how to flesh out. Do what you can, take a break, and then add to it.

Bonus: Rent one of the movies discussed in this chapter and watch it while armed with a pad of paper and something to write with. Look for each plot point and note when it occurs. Watch the setup before each plot point, and the aftermath surrounding it. Pause and rewind where necessary. Study how the movie flows from plot point to plot point. Repeat this analysis each time you watch a movie, or read a book, until it becomes second nature.

If you're not into movies pick an old favorite book and perform the same plot point analysis.

Exercise #11- The First Part of the Circle

Go back and read the document you created in exercise #10. Now create a new document and label it The Story Circle. Add the following:

1. You
2. Need
3. Go
4. Road of Trials
5. Meet the Goddess
6. Take & Pay
7. Return
8. Changed

Write a full paragraph for You that includes your character's passion, as well as the flaw that arises from it. Repeat this process for Need. What event is propelling your character into the story? Finally, add Go. What's the point of no return for your hero?

These descriptions should build on what you created in the previous document, and the goal is to examine your story from multiple angles to see what that jars loose in your subconscious.

Bonus: If you've got the time, re-watch or re-read the first act of the movie / book you picked in the last exercise. This time you're looking to see if it follows the story circle. What did you pick up this time that you might have missed when watching it, thinking about the three-act structure?

Exercise #12- The Second Part of the Circle

Open the story circle document from the last chapter. Under the Road of Trials section, brainstorm three scenes that will bring your character closer to their goal from Need. What trials do they need to face? How are those trials affected by their flaws, and what lessons does this force your character to learn? What external force is propelling them forward?

Define each of these with as much detail as you can muster. It won't all be clear just yet, but hopefully you have some rough ideas.

Now move to the Meet the Goddess step. How can you grant your character what they think they wanted, but also show that they really wanted something else? Consider Star Wars, The Matrix, and Dawn of the Dead and how they did it. Look to your favorite stories. How are they doing it?

Now craft a scene or scenes that will force your character to accept responsibility. They will pass from the passive into the active side of the story circle. They're taking ownership, and actively working to become the person they need to be.

Consider which characters you could add to your plot to fulfill both of these plot points. Who will your protagonist meet? Allies? A mentor? This is your opportunity to add one or more characters.

Bonus: Continue your re-watch / re-read from the last chapter. Watch up to the midpoint of the movie until you've seen / read the Meet the Goddess phase. Did you spot anything that you didn't when analyzing the book for the three-act structure?

~

Exercise #13- The Third Part of the Circle

Get out your story circle document, and add your Take & Pay. What is all this going to cost your heroine? What does she lose? Does this require you to add a setup earlier in the book? Modify the earlier sections of the document if needed.

If you remember from the LAYER step, we added a Return. Compare the original with your ending in the three-act document. After reading both, write your Return step using what you've read in this chapter. What is the final confrontation? And how can you make things look their bleakest, just before the inevitable victory in Changed?

Now add your Changed step, and bring it all together. This is the ultimate payoff that you first envisioned back in the LAYER step. Are you offering a satisfying conclusion? Are you paying off all the setups? Most importantly, has your character transformed into the heroine they need to be?

Bonus: Finish your re-watch / re-read. Open a fresh document, and write out your thoughts about the story. Did it follow the story circle? Were you able to spot all the plot points? Pick a book or movie you think is bad, and perform exactly the same kind of analysis. Where do they mess up and why?

∽

Exercise #14- Outline Your Novel

This is the big one. We've gradually given you all the basic tools necessary to outline your novel. Take every document you've created and arrange them into either the three-act structure or the story circle as shown in my screenshot above. It's totally okay (and expected) for there to be gaps at this point.

Go through every single document and lay out the scene using the technique in this chapter. Where does it take place? Who is the PoV character? What type of scene is it? Add the corresponding letter to your scene.

I highly recommend doing the bonus step as well. This exercise might only be a couple hundred words long, but what I'm asking you to do can be a monumental undertaking. It may mean weeks of adding documents and changing descriptions.

That's totally okay. Your outline is a living, breathing thing that will change over time. All you're doing here is completing the first draft.

Bonus: Consider the needs of your genre. Do you have enough A scenes? Do you have 1-2 Rs? Do you need more Ss? Tweak your outline to include these additional scenes.

Once you're finished, read the outline from the top. How does it sound?

Exercise #15- Add a Plot Branch

Add three plot branches to your Take & Pay step. What if the story veered off in another direction? Consider ways it could go very badly, or humorously, or favorably. Which fits the tone of the book you're after? Which best informs the character you're creating?

Modify the outline to include the changes.

Bonus: Repeat this process with your Return step. Create a reminder for one week. Re-read all versions you've created, then re-write one final version.

Exercise #16- Cultivate Some Characters

Go through your entire outline and generate a working list of characters for your novel in your format of choice. I use the Character section of Scrivener for this, but if Index cards work for you, that's fine. Anything that generates a complete list is acceptable.

Make a list of labels or symbols associated with each character. Are they tall? Are they a know-it-all? Consider each character. Then, and only then, go out and find artwork for each and drop it into the file, or print it out if you're doing analogue.

Set a reminder for tomorrow at an appropriate time. Review each character, and take a moment to stare at each image you downloaded. Say the character's name out loud as you're staring at the image.

This process will force your brain to create a sort of person symbol for each character, making them just as real as the people you actually know.

Bonus: Write a paragraph in each character file from the perspective of the character. What does their dialogue sound like? What concerns do they have on a daily basis? How are they different from you?

Exercise #17- The Last One

If you are planning on writing a series, then choose a type. Are you writing an epic, or a series of standalone novels? If it's standalones, have a high five and skip this exercise. If it's an epic, then put on your gloves because we're about to do some gardening.

Spend a moment considering the epic ending of your series. What might it look like? This is just a thought experiment, and is likely to change several times. For now, just pick something that sounds cool, and run with it. Will your character conquer the world? Become president? Get her own talk show and become bigger than Oprah?

Once you have an idea, think about the timeframe. How far away is this hypothetical future? A year? Five? Sixty? Pick something appropriate to your genre and setting. How might your character change between now and then? Who will they have to become, and what will they have to master to be this dream version of themselves? Start jotting down notes on their character sheet.

Now take a look at your cast as a whole. How will the existing cast develop over the series? Repeat the process with each of them until you have a rough idea of how each will grow and change throughout the series.

Bonus: Pick a long-running series in the same genre as your novel, ideally one you haven't read. Start reading it. As you do so, take special note of each protagonist in the novel, and when you finish each book take the time to write down how you think each grew or changed. Did you find that growth satisfying? Which characters do you like?

Repeat this until you've done a case study on every book in the series. How did the author handle their character arcs? Did the series sustain your interest? Why or why not?

Made in the USA
Columbia, SC
11 May 2018